MONTANA
DUCK HUNTING TALES

MONTANA
DUCK HUNTING TALES

MATT WEMPLE

THE
History
PRESS

Published by The History Press
Charleston, SC
www.historypress.com

Copyright © 2024 by Matt Wemple
All rights reserved

All photographs courtesy of the author unless otherwise noted.

Opposite: Fighting the muck, Red Rock Lakes National Wildlife Refuge.
Jamie Young.

First published 2024

Manufactured in the United States

ISBN 9781467157605

Library of Congress Control Number: 2024941859

Dedicated to Eugene Alex Betz,
with whom I shared some of my best days in a Montana duck blind.

1970–2021

CONTENTS

ACKNOWLEDGEMENTS

No author ever writes alone. There is always help somewhere along the way. The following family, friends and colleagues were indispensable in bringing this work to fruition, and I am indebted to them.

Lisa Wemple
John and Lulu Wemple
Don and Linda Page
Alex Betz
Jamie Young
Wade Hill
Adam Pankratz
Justin Hawkaluk
Amos and Ethan Ridenour
Kevin Murphy
Jay Hanson
James Alfred Hanson
E. Donnall Thomas Jr.

Dan Cook
Dale Spartas
Bob Morton
Mark Schlepp
Claire Gower
Jim and Phyllis Hansen
Jeff Herbert
Dennis Hagenston
Roger Parker
Dusty Emond
Ben Morin
Andy Matakis

INTRODUCTION

As a waterfowl hunting state, Montana offers a lot. It doesn't advertise this or get the notoriety other states do. It is a big state, the fourth largest in the nation. It holds a sizeable portion of two flyways, the Central and the Pacific. It is blessed with an abundance of intact wetland habitat, from the base of mountain ranges to across the vast prairie. These wetlands labor to produce ducks through the summer breeding season as well as provide hunting opportunities come fall. Montana is a land of rivers. Once marshes freeze over, rivers hold ducks. Unlike many western states, Montana has a stream access law very friendly to sportsmen. Hunting opportunities abound wherever waders allow you to walk between the ordinary high-water marks.

Relative to duck marshes across the rest of the United States, hunting pressure in Montana is rather light. Favored hunting grounds near booming population centers can be a bit crowded on opening weekend. After that, pressure in any form fizzles out quickly. The reason? Every weekend past the opener, a new, different hunting season opens, pulling most would-be waterfowlers in other directions. Upland birds and big game peel off most of the competition, leaving many duck haunts quiet and available. With the surge of new residents the state is experiencing now, the competition for access to private land has heated up. But it's still possible with the state's block management program, and there is still a lot of public access in Montana compared to the rest of the country.

Fall migration, Pacific Flyway.

To hunt waterfowl in Montana is to learn the story of wildlife conservation as it occurred here. Montana as a state was at the forefront of the wildlife conservation movement in the early twentieth century. It beat most other states to the punch in the latter half of the nineteenth century by establishing game laws and deputizing game wardens to enforce them. As things progressed, it began to set aside habitat for wildlife, including wetlands, of which it has an abundance. As Montana's rivers course through mountain valleys and onto the prairie where the western edge of the Prairie Pothole Region starts, there are numerous state wildlife management areas, national wildlife refuges and waterfowl production areas.

When I got to Montana over twenty years ago, I knew I'd do some duck hunting, but I didn't realize how much. From the time I arrived, I saw ducks everywhere I went. Mallards! Lots of 'em. In the Pacific Flyway, where I now live, the season runs significantly longer than on the rest of the continent. It begins somewhere around the end of September or beginning of October, depending on the year, and runs till about mid-January. As I discovered, that meant once the general big game rifle season was over, I had a month and a half of waterfowl hunting left! On top of that, the limit was seven ducks a day—and as of this writing, it still is!

What makes duck hunting here so much fun is accessibility. I didn't have to drive far, and I didn't need a boat to get to the ducks. Within twenty minutes of home, I could be stepping into a river with a shotgun and a decoy sack. I thought I'd died and gone to heaven. Watching fat December mallards cup their wings and descend to my small spread of seven or eight decoys through a wall of lightly falling snow was magical. The more I explored duck hunting in Montana, the more I realized I'd never experience everything she has to offer in a lifetime. But I've sure tried. What follows this introduction is a journey along Montana's waterfowl hunting trail. From the mountains to the prairies, we explore its diverse landscape where good waterfowl hunting can be found. Along the way, we find unique history and people and lots of ducks under a big sky.

CHAPTER 1

ALONG THE EASTERN FRONT

Cresting the lip of the Fairfield Bench, the prairie dropped away to the horizon in shades of green and tan as native grasses interspersed cut rows of barley. It was early October. The oblique autumn sunlight shimmered off a giant sliver of water surrounded by wetland pockets sprawling north along the slope of the bench. Rising above, the eastern slope of the Rocky Mountain Front spanned the horizon, a fresh skiff of snow across the top. The sliver of water was Freezout Lake.

Freezout is a legend among Montana's dedicated waterfowlers. I first hunted here with my close friend avid waterfowler Alex Betz in the fall of 2009. Alex and I met in the army, spending much of our "hurry up and wait" time talking duck hunting. The mention of Freezout would cause him to get this bright but faraway look in his eyes. It evoked a wave of emotion and memories that really meant something. Alex has hunted Freezout since his college days in Missoula. Some of his fondest hunting memories were made here. All else being equal, when things are good here, they are as good as duck hunting gets anywhere.

With the right weather, ducks pile into this place. Alex hunted here with Molly, his first Lab, a yellow. He believes she was *that* dog—that once-in-a-lifetime dog that no matter how hard you try, you'll never own another like it. Her eyes never left the sky and locked onto ducks instantly. Here, Alex and Molly watched some of the most spectacular sunrises he can remember. With close friends, he hunted the first big fronts of the year, pushing through while everyone else was hunting elk in the mountains. Good mornings brought limits fast. I heard these stories over and over again until I'd heard enough, and we planned a trip. Arriving there a day early, I had my own Lab at my side, Roxy. It was her first hunt.

DUCK SEASON STARTED THE next day. Our first day, we planned to scout things out from a distance to see what we might expect in the morning. Ron, the senior member of our trio, had driven in all the way from Idaho to get a crack at opening day birds. Unable to wait any longer, he took off early that first morning, beating me and Alex by a couple of hours. From the parking area, there are several foot access points into the core of the wildlife management area (WMA), where you'll find the main lake, several satellite ponds and wetland areas along the lakeshore, courtesy of a Ducks Unlimited (DU) project in the '80s. Roxy barreled down the trail, tuning her senses to the sights, sounds and smells that mean only one thing: it's time to hunt.

Thus far, it had been a warm fall. Ducks weren't piling in yet, but birds were there. Scanning the far-flung pockets of the lake through binoculars, I could see small pods of ducks here and there. Teal, gadwall, wigeon and a few mallards made up the species list so far. The great thing about Freezout, a funneling point of the Pacific and Central Flyways, is that one never knows what might swing into the decoys. Anything is possible. Snow geese wouldn't be there for a while yet. However, ducks were there, and we'd been anticipating this day since mid-January.

A crown jewel of Montana's wildlife management areas, Freezout Lake was established in 1953. Its beginnings date to the late 1920s, when the Fairfield Bench/Greenfield Irrigation District sought to use the natural basin Freezout sits in as a collection point for irrigation runoff. This was already an area that naturally held water, and it soon became apparent that water, once here, wouldn't go anywhere. After a point, there was too much water, and local farmlands and roads saw significant flooding. The Irrigation District, along with the Bureau of Reclamation, developed a plan in the early 1950s to drain the lake and make things more tenable for local farmers.[*]

The end result was a system of dykes that would drain water into nearby Priest Lake and, eventually, the Teton River. At the same time, Montana Fish, Wildlife and Parks became very interested in establishing a WMA here. With the drainage system in place, six ponds were constructed around the main lake, connected with head gates, which enabled adjusting of water

_____

[*] Wemple, "Schlepp," 1.

Shooting distance estimator station, Freezout Lake Wildlife Management Area.

levels. This allows area managers to maintain a wetland environment that benefits many species. With a surrounding environment prone to many instabilities, Freezout maintains a stable ecosystem, which helps ensure waterfowl complete their annual migration.[*]

The area around Freezout Lake has always been in a natural migration corridor, as waterfowl have long used the spine of the continent as a highway south. There are two things ducks and geese need on their trip south to make it: a good restaurant and a decent hotel halfway there. Freezout is both. The area around Fairfield is one of the largest grain-producing areas in the country. It's no accident that the grain silo complex in town has been owned by both Anheuser-Busch and Coors at one time or another. The vast surrounding barley fields combined with a large wetland complex create the ideal stopping point between the arctic and points south.

Not long after establishment of the WMA, snow geese from all major flyways learned Freezout was an ideal resting spot along the annual migration

---

[*] Wemple, "Schlepp," 2.

route and begin to congregate annually in epic numbers, fall and spring. This is perhaps the one event Freezout is most noted for. More than anything, it's the food supply that draws them in. The added benefit of water seals the deal. In the late 1950s, WMA staff began to notice the uptick in snow goose presence. A literal tornado of geese dropping into the lake can be seen when the migration peaks. This is the main event that gives Freezout its notoriety.

Additionally, tundra swans gain attention—from the lucky hunters who draw a permit. As it's the barley that brings the snows in, it is the aquatic vegetation and invertebrates teeming in the lake that attract swans. Tundra swans began using Freezout as a stopover about the same time as snow geese. The soft clay bottom, different from those of other area lakes, supports a smorgasbord of this swan-preferred fare.

Duck numbers can fluctuate a bit, more than do snow geese or swans. If moisture conditions are good in a given year, ducks will disperse more across the flyways and not funnel into the area as they might in a dry year, but this is true of any duck-hunting area. Ducks do consistently show up, albeit in varying numbers.

Early the next morning Alex, Ron and I pulled on waders, fed dogs, loaded decoy sacks on the game cart, shouldered shotguns and headed to the DU ponds near the eastern lakeshore. Ron, not wanting to slog through the muck, opted to hunt on the lakeshore, while Alex and I trudged through the tules and cattails to a pond we'd eyeballed the evening prior. Temps were in the forties, and the sky was overcast. A front was due to push through sometime during opening weekend but seemed to have been held up at the Canadian border.

With the pond deked out, we tucked into the cattails to await shooting time. After we ripped out a few mallard hen calls, two gadwall dropped in. In Alex's shot lane, he scored a double as they cupped and swung down. Cassie, Alex's Chesapeake Bay retriever, darted off on a dead run, fetching both birds back to us. Small pods of ducks dotted the lake as dawn broke. Soon, we heard Ron shooting over by the lakeshore. We couldn't see him, but we saw birds falling from the air over his blind. Our next shots came at green-wings buzzing low over the pond. We hit two or three as they buzzed over the top of the grass. They flew so low and fast, it was hard to track them. As to who killed what, it's a moot point. That's why duck hunting is intended to be done with friends. If somebody claims a bird, let 'em have it. Maybe they did shoot it. Maybe they need it more than you.

Our morning's take was turning out to be typical of duck hunting at Freezout: diverse. In Alex's words, a brown bag special: mallard, gadwall,

Anheuser-Busch grain elevators, Fairfield, Montana.

green-wing teal and one pintail. Things slowed down significantly about midmorning. We still had a few birds to go till our limit. About noon, things kicked up again. We cheered watching a Canada fall to Ron's shotgun—first honker of the season. Ron did well to hunt the lakeshore. Teal buzzed him all morning, some larger ducks mixed in—then to top things off, a stray Canada! Sometimes things just seem to work out better for the old guys. They deserve some easy birds, as they've already paid their dues. It wasn't until the afternoon that I thought about it, but other than the three of us, I'd heard no gunfire in the immediate vicinity.

Overcrowding at Freezout is seldom a problem. The size of the area and the fact that birds are generally distributed throughout seems to keep hunters spread out. Most of the crowding occurs with locals on the levees who prefer to pass shoot without decoys. Get out in the grass around the lake, and you seem to have your pick of spots. The campground can fill up on opening weekend, but after that, things taper off significantly. The arrival of snow geese can offset this but only slightly. Other than that, most hunters will have much of the WMA to themselves. Freezout is also a good distance from major population centers, Great Falls being the nearest at an hour away. The town of Fairfield is a stone's throw, with all the basic needs of any hunter: grocery store, hardware (think ammo), etc.

Freezout is more than just a hunting area, says Mark Schlepp, retired Freezout WMA manager. It's a world-class birding destination. While the numbers of birders hardly eclipse those of hunters, the birders who do come here travel from much farther away than the hunters, who are mostly from within Montana. Mark has met folks from all over the United States and even as far away as Europe hoping to glimpse a snow goose tornado or a tundra swan in flight. And then there's the less common recreationist group of windsurfers, which makes perfect sense to anyone who's experienced an average day's wind on the Front.

Wind in this area at times can top seventy miles per hour, with gusts of up to one hundred. Alex was headed home from Freezout one fall day with such winds. Molly was riding in the back of his slide-in pickup camper. All was going well—until he looked back and saw the pickup camper wasn't there. It got sucked out of the pickup bed and deposited in the median along I-15. Molly was found safe and sound inside, and the camper sustained only minor damage—still, a testament to the strength of Montana wind.

Main entrance to Freezout Lake Wildlife Management Area.

What goes largely unknown is the quiet but professional work that goes into keeping a finger on the pulse of the WMA and monitoring its health. Overall, Freezout Lake maintains a clean bill in that regard. A variety of factors play into this: soil content, low selenium levels in the water and plain old good luck, among other things. Soil and water conditions play heavily into the health of any wetland. Freezout is blessed with all the good stuff. Nearby Benton Lake Refuge north of Great Falls has suffered from high selenium in recent times. High selenium levels in a wetland can cause sterilization of the water, leading to birth defects in birds. While Freezout's water health is in good shape, much of it is dependent upon the ability to alter water levels, which mitigates high selenium levels.[*]

Some critical habitat work in the 1980s cosponsored by DU helped expand wetlands along the edges of the lake. The initial intent was to dig a canal in a Z pattern and flood water into it to create more wetland areas along the lake. The purpose of the Z canal was to improve brood survival among ducks in spring. Ducks by nature are very territorial, and the legs of the Z canals provide each brood its own area to thrive in, reducing their interference in one another's territories. A huge side benefit came from the water pumped into the canal, which created residual wetland habitat in and around the lake. The very pond Alex and I were hunting resulted from this project.

Wildlife, in general, is abundant around Freezout. In addition to avian residents, deer and pronghorn inhabit the surrounding bench country. Predators such as coyotes, skunks, raccoon and foxes proliferate as well. Freezout does welcome coyote hunters and fur trappers through winter. More recently, grizzly bears have taken a shine to the area. Absent from the prairie for a century, they have become increasingly common as their population expands and younger bears get pushed out of the Rocky Mountain Front. Elk show up on occasion as well. That such a diverse suite of wildlife is attracted to the area speaks to the quality of the habitat.

Alex and I piled into the truck with the dogs to do some windshield scouting. As we drove up and down US 89, which bisects the WMA between Choteau and Fairfield, Alex got that faraway look in his eye. He began to relive a hunt from the mid-'90s.

"Man, we had a hunt that day. It was opening weekend and had probably been in the seventies the day before opener. We were walking around camp in shorts! I'd come in from Missoula and went back to stay with my folks in

---

[*] Wemple, "Schlepp," 3.

Great Falls. So I'm getting up the next morning, and I step out the door. There's three inches of fresh snow on the ground, and it's still coming down! I'm in a hurry to get here and do some sliding on the road on the way here.

"My buddy Chad and I along with about six other dudes from Missoula were hunting together. The weather threw us off, so we were a little behind the power curve on getting set up. We headed out into the DU ponds to hunt, and at daylight, we saw ducks flying everywhere. Mallards, canvasbacks, you name it: ducks everywhere. We really didn't need decoys. The shooting started, and everybody was killing ducks. One thing we'd forgotten about was breakfast. Chad ran back to get a hibachi grill and brought it out to the blind.

"So we've nearly limited out, and now Chad is cooking up some of our birds on the grill. Right about the time he's flipping duck breasts, I see a lone drake can coming in. 'He's coming to dinner!' I shout out loud. I shoot, and he falls stone-dead right in front of the hibachi. I dress him out and toss him over to Chad.

"I bet you that hunt didn't last longer than an hour, and we were limited out. Wave after wave kept coming in. We piled the birds up for a photo. With eight dudes hunting, there must have been a few shy of fifty ducks piled up in that picture. What a day!"

Alex's gaze was transfixed on the ponds we were scouting as he stared into the past.

"Well, the forecast is looking a little nasty for tomorrow. I don't know about fifty birds on the ground, but we might have some luck," I said as we bounced down the gravel road to check out the impoundments north of the lake. One had the most birds on the far end of it today, so our plan was to hunt there in the morning.

The weather we hoped for finally arrived. Better day two of opening weekend than never. In the predawn darkness, we loaded dogs into the pickup as flurries swirled in a biting north wind. Such weather stirs a duck hunter's soul. Based on our windshield scouting the day before, we settled on a pond off the main lake. Birds were holding to the far side of it, but maybe the weather would move them a little. Hopefully a few new birds would show up. True to form, birds were on the move. Local birds remained wary, but new birds provided some shooting. We drank coffee and ate doughnuts during the lulls. Life is tough out there. As I lifted my cup to my lips, a wigeon buzzed out front of the blind, and Alex folded it with one shot. It fell and got blown out to sea by a sudden gale. Cassie sprang into action and made a hundred-yard retrieve, fetching the bird before it blew out of sight.

Alex Betz and
Lab Molly on a
hunt at Freezout
Lake, 2002.

The hunt continued apace. We collected another brown bag special that morning with a good early fall complement of puddlers. They made a good meal. Best of all, we had the water to ourselves. That seems to be the routine on opening weekend at Freezout. Like ducks on opening weekend, hunters pile in on opening morning and raft up at home on day two, not moving or going anywhere. Ducks weren't blackening the skies that day, but they were there. The weather turning helped move a few more around. It's hard to beat duck hunting on opening weekend. It's mostly about knocking the rust off and fine-tuning your routine for the season. Add to that the surroundings of Freezout, and does it really matter how many ducks get shot? For Alex, it was all about coming home after being gone for too long. I counted myself lucky to be with him.

CHAPTER 2

BANDED CREEK

Discovery is a large part of what leads many to hunt. It is discovery that leads you around the next bend in the river, over the next ridge—and if you're doing it right, through life itself. Near my home in southwest Montana runs a stream that, on maps at least, has no name. It could be considered a braid of the Madison River. Given how long it flows away from the river, though, and the fact that it runs on a dual source—both the river and warm springs welling up from the ground—it may as well be its own stream. I found it during my second duck season out west, not long after my wife, Lisa, and I moved out to Three Forks.

In early December my second season here, I found myself hunting among the Madison's braided channels not far outside town. After a couple of hunts, I got a good idea where the ducks liked to be. I never hauled out limits but always had two- to three-bird days on average, good enough for a dinner or two. The temp was somewhere in the mid-twenties and felt like it was dropping. I'd seen a few birds on the wing but nothing receptive to my decoys or calls. I did notice, as late morning came on, that the ducks seemed to be heading north and descending below a line of cottonwoods.

It was a mystery to me why they were dropping in there, and I decided to find out. Wading across several more stream braids, I arrived at the river's main channel. An ice shelf extended about four feet out from my side of the bank. Straight across the river from me was a steep cutbank. Easing out to the edge of the ice shelf, I broke through, landing in knee-deep water. An easy wade, it got shallow up against the cutbank. Just up from there, across fifty yards of private ground, steam wafted into the air. Staying legal, I walked the bank downriver. Ahead, I could see a channel branching off from the main river. I hoped it led to where all those mallards had been going. I walked down the creek, which was bolstered by cutbanks on either side, the right much shorter than the left. Up ahead, I could see another stream channel joining this one, steam coming off and not a trace of ice in it. Then I heard hens' quacking mixed with the low humming of drake mallards and geese honking!

Staying low, I crept along below the cutbank, finally getting to a spot where I could see over to the source of the steam. A long, wide slough stretched out before me, covered bank to bank with a sea of green heads mixed in with the intermittent gray bodies of Canada geese. My head barely peeking over the top sent thirty or so birds airborne. This didn't spook what was probably several hundred ducks covering the slough. Ducking back down, I watched the flight circle around and land on the far side of the slough. The sight alone had been worth the walk. I just sat there, listening. It's not often you get a chance to hear such diverse waterfowl language. When you get this close to a bunch of them, you hear every sound they make.

I eased forward to see how close I could get. Of course, my camera was in the dry bag next to the decoys back in the brush across the river. I'd gotten maybe three feet out past the cutbank when they became aware of my presence. In a roar of splashing, wingbeats, quacks and honks, the birds vacated the slough with amazing speed. The sudden rush of air among their collective wings sounded similar to a wind gust. Awestruck, I watched as several flights began to circle back. Coming to my senses, I readied the 870 and scored two birds out of a flight cupped to come in. At that, the skies cleared, and all went silent. Gathering my two birds off the water, I explored further. For a good two to three hundred yards, this creek meandered along with little to no ice due to the warm spring source. I'd hit pay dirt.

Mom and Dad came in for a visit on Christmas Day. Dad and I went straight to the Broken Spur Motel to get his license and duck stamps. The next morning, we stepped off the levee into the slushy Madison River. This was Dad's first time ever hunting up north. For his first hunt, it wasn't too cold, maybe thirty above. I took him to the braided channels just off the levee first to start him off easy. Last night's snow covered everything in a powdery blanket. I threw out a few dekes, and we settled into our basic blind of willow and cattail, awaiting shooting time. We sipped coffee. Dad was processing that we'd waded through an icy river in the dark, snow falling through our headlamp beams and snow on the ground, then set up in a makeshift blind, all within a short walk of the truck. He had to pinch himself. I'll admit I felt much the same the more I thought about it.

The first bird to come in was a lone mallard drake. It lit in the dekes and dabbled around a bit. I motioned to Dad that if he wanted to jump him out of the dekes and take a shot, he could. Dad eased into position. He'd barely made a move before that drake was airborne and out of range, before he could shoot. Dad wasn't used to ducks decoying like that and landing right in front of you. It just didn't happen in the midst of Louisiana public land combat duck hunting.

I told Dad he had to let the birds decoy and come in. Once the drama played out and they were committed, then it was time to pick out a bird and shoot. It took restraint on his part, but he finally got to where he enjoyed just watching the birds work as much as the shooting. Eventually, more birds were flying, and finally we got some to bag, mallards mostly and one goldeneye, Dad's first. We even had a flight of geese come within range. In excitement and surprise, we blew that opportunity. Don't ask me how—just one of those things. Our hunting experience together crossed into a new realm for him this morning.

Our next hunt was New Year's Eve morning. I took him to the spring creek. Dad didn't really get the significance of what we were about to do because he hadn't seen what I had. Even better, the mercury had dropped to around fifteen degrees, making a hunting spot like this a real good situation. On our walk in, we were greeted by a cacophony of wingbeats, splashes, quacks and honks. Who knows how many birds took to the air, no doubt spooked by our sloshing and headlamp beams. With nearly all still water in the valley locked up and rivers starting to freeze over, the birds didn't have many options. We set up well before dawn. At shooting time, mallards were coming in. They buzzed in through the falling snow all around us. We cut three birds from the first flight. Reloading and visually checking our spread, we prepared for the next one. Dad watched the skies intently as I alternated feeding and drake calls.

I waded out to flip a deke right-side up and brush snow off the rest. While I did so, Dad's shotgun thumped behind me. Turning around, I watched as a mallard drake folded and spiraled, nearly whacking Dad's gun barrel. It snuck in from behind, making a distinct thud as it smacked into the bank. "Whew, that was close!" Dad said as I waded back to our makeshift blind and hunkered down. We'd cleared a little over a one-man limit when things slowed down. I began piling up the ducks to take stock of the morning's success. I picked up the one mallard hen Dad shot and brushed the snow off her. When I flipped her over and checked her feet, I saw a band! Don't know how we missed that!

This was the first banded bird either of us had taken. "Speechless" and "ecstatic" might describe our feelings in that moment. This is a big deal in duck hunting, no matter where you are. With eight fat mallards, the game strap felt hefty. Dad draped it around his neck just to experience the weight of those eight grain-fattened Montana mallards. Holding it made my bicep tense up a little. We would have hunted longer, but we had to meet our wives for brunch. So we waded back to the truck as the snow fell. We couldn't stop talking about the band.

Mom and Dad flew home the next day. Dad not being one for taxidermy, I made him a lanyard with the band crimped around tail feathers from the hen and several of the birds in that day's bag. Two days later, I headed back out to hunt the spring creek. The weather had gotten colder.

The morning was calm and clear, and as I left town, the bank thermometer read a flat zero. My pulse quickened knowing the birds would be on the move. Late season conditions were in full swing. Ice shelves were stretching ever farther over the stream channels. My waders were covered in a thin sheet of ice. I arrived at the spring creek with faint hints of dawn coming, late this time of year. With the decoys out, I settled in against the bank with willows for overhead cover. I blew maybe two notes on my call, then heard quacks in every direction. Soon, ducks bombed into my spread of seven decoys. So many ducks piled into the water, I couldn't possibly keep count. It was as if a spigot had been turned on and ducks began pouring out. My best guess was over a hundred. I'd never experienced anything like this, ever. In awe of the moment, I didn't even shoot. I simply watched. The ducks kept coming and coming.

I thought of Dad, who, only feet from me two days ago, was now two thousand miles away. God, how I wished he was here to see this. Ducks were dabbling and making all manner of racket feet from me. Seeing their winged silhouettes descend backlit by the dawn left me awestruck. After taking in this spectacle, I readied my gun for the next flight that would swing in. At my first shots, a riot of wings erupted. To my astonishment, after I'd shot a couple, the ones that left kept coming back! Ducks kept coming and kept coming. As I watched the ducks work in all directions, their sounds were shut out by the honks of geese flying along the creek. As the flight of low-flying Canadas passed, I scored a double, my first ever.

I had four mallards and two geese on the ground next to me. I knew I could easily get a limit if I just held out. For some reason, though, I told myself that five birds with two geese would be good enough. I decided I would shoot one more mallard and call it a morning. A drake came in and worked over the decoys. Folding him on the first shot, I waded out to pick him up. I checked his feet. He had a band! Dad and I had both shot our first banded ducks in the same spot within two days of each other. At that moment, I didn't feel alone anymore. He may have been far away, but as I rotated that band around the drake's orange-red leg, I felt Dad smiling right next to me. I hadn't mounted a single duck in my life yet. Here was a good first candidate. Rolling a stocking over the bird to keep his feathers straight, I carefully placed him in the decoy bag atop the heavy load of dekes, ducks and geese.

Post-hunt, I called in both band numbers to the U.S. Fish and Wildlife Service. It used to be you had to send in the band to get a data card back on the bird. As banded birds came to mean something very special to duck hunters, the agency eventually changed this policy. In about a month, our banding information cards arrived in the mail. My drake was born in 2002 or earlier. It was banded seven miles east of Mirror, Alberta. Mirror is a tiny hamlet about halfway between Calgary and Edmonton. Just east sits Buffalo Lake and a ton of smaller lakes and ponds. On a map, it looks like pothole central—a good place for a mallard to be.

Dad's bird took the cake as far as journeys go. His hen, hatched in 2003, was banded northwest of Yellowknife, Northwest Territories, smack-dab between Nunavut and the Yukon—about as wild as wild country gets in the world. This would place the duck somewhere in the vicinity of a long, northwest-pointing arm of Great Slave Lake. The country in this area is a transition zone from boreal forest to tundra. This duck would have had to avoid host of predators: arctic foxes, wolverines, grizzly bears and wolves, to name a few. All that to contend with, and she met her fate near the headwaters of the Missouri!

Later that spring, I met a unique individual I'd get to know more over the years, Jeff Waldum. Jeff specializes in bird taxidermy and, at the time, made his home south of Livingston. A teacher on the full-time side, Jeff is a passionate hunter and taxidermist. He treats each customer like a client. He wants to meet you and get to know you and your bird. We met for coffee one sunny February day in Bozeman. Jeff carried a portfolio of his work, which provided insight into how I might have the drake posed. I had a pretty good idea of what I wanted, but his photos helped me fine-tune some details. In my mind, the "wings cupped, landing gear down" pose was the only way to go.

Jeff, working strictly with birds, only takes on the amount of work his part-time schedule allows. This means he has a pretty quick turnaround time. I

First banded duck.

dropped the bird off in mid-February, and by late April, it was done! Even better was the fact that Mom and Dad happened to be up for another visit, and Dad got to be there with me when I picked it up. The mount looked phenomenal. I was so happy. The spring creek where Dad and I shot these ducks has no name and likely never will—not on a map, anyway. After the hunt Dad and I had there, I felt it deserved one, at least in our own minds. "Banded Creek" seemed fitting. I hunted this spot many times in the coming years: sometimes with friends, most times alone. It was on these solo hunts that the special nature of this place came alive. This creek was little more than a mile from the nearest road.

One morning, while sipping coffee on its banks, I looked up from my cup to see a young bull moose browsing on willow branches, a mat of frost on his back. He looked at me, then went back to eating. Nearly every hunt, a lone kingfisher would flitter through and take his perch on a buffaloberry branch overhanging a sharp bend in the creek. In the skeletal branches of a tall cottonwood, high above all, a lone bald eagle would perch sometimes in the morning, right after daybreak. Muskrats swam along the banks—and on one occasion, an otter. This nook of habitat overflowed with wildlife. The more I hunted it, the more it grew on me. There were days when hunting was slow. But the creek always had something to offer that was good.

CHAPTER 3

DUCKS BELOW ZERO

The air hung dense and frozen along the edge of the warm spring slough. Steam wafted off its surface as daylight crept along the bleak, arctic-like horizon. The bolt slammed shut as I chambered shell number three in the twelve-gauge Browning Gold. The night before, knowing the temps would be somewhere around minus twenty this morning, I made sure to break it down and remove any trace of excess lubricant. In this weather, it tends to gel and slow things up when you don't need it to. Roxy, my black Lab, looked up at me as the bolt closed, then turned her intent gaze back to the slough and the horizon. When the mercury heads south of zero and the hunter can get to open water, ducks come in quick and in large numbers around here.

The sound of wings cutting air descended through the overhanging willows. I watched a pod of eight wigeon drop in. They snuck in right behind me. With the likelihood of more birds following close behind and a few minutes left until legal shooting time, I held tight. Roxy let out a soft whimper. A gentle squeeze on her scruff got her to quiet down. Another flight came in from my left, then another from behind. Pintails! I could hear their soft peeping whistles before I saw them. This was going to be a good day. The slough was beginning to fill up. Soon it would be time for the first shot. I drew a bead on a bull sprig, cupped and preparing to drop down into the other birds milling about on the water.

My first shot was a miss. "Get your damn cheek on the stock!" I told myself. He was a nice sprig with a super-long tail feather. At the first shot, the slough erupted in a flurry of wingbeats and myriad sounds of multiple duck species taking flight in abrupt panic. I dropped two wigeon stone-dead. Roxy fetched them to the bank in short order. I wasn't too worried about all those ducks taking off. On cold days like this, the birds don't have a lot of other places to go. If you're in the right spot, they'll keep coming back.

Less than three minutes later, that's just what they did: mallards this time, big fat greenheads. Scoring another double, I reloaded, as more were inbound on the horizon. Roxy busted through the ice on the bank bringing one of the drakes back, then headed back out for the other one. As she brought the second one back, I motioned her to the brown carpet square next to the propane heater. With four birds down, we were on track to finish early. Even though the flights slowed down over the course of the morning, we managed to limit out by nine o'clock. While such conditions are harsh, hunting on days like this is worth it.

We capitalized on the shock of the weather. Two days before, an arctic air mass descended on Montana, gripping much of the state in a deep freeze. Within twenty-four hours, any vestige of open water sealed shut and local rivers filled with slush. Soon they, too, would freeze, gorged with ice. In parts of the state farther north, the mercury dipped to forty below zero. When this happens, the combined effect of any open water left freezing up along with fresh birds pushed down by the front produces some of the best duck shooting hunters will see all season, provided they are prepared to act on it.

Twenty years have passed since my first Montana duck season, my introduction to hunting in subzero weather. I learned a lot the first season— the hard way. And while the details of more recent seasons can blur, one into the next, the hunts that first season remain etched in my mind like scrimshaw. The snow fell in waving sheets as thick white exhaust poured out the pipes of my '91 F-250, warming up on the street. I watched through the window, sipping the first cup of coffee. Getting in the truck, I made the short drive down to the Gallatin River. Arriving at the fishing access site, I slipped on waders, shouldered half a dozen decoys and the Remington 870 and made my way to the river as the snow slacked off a little. With the onset of shooting time, a pair of mallards buzzed overhead. A quick high-ball on the hen call and they circled right back, dropping into my spread. It happened so textbook I almost didn't believe it. This almost never happened in the high-pressure duck holes of Louisiana. I scored a double, my first Montana mallards. Legal shooting time that day was about 7:40 or so. December daylight comes late and goes early this far north.

That first week in December, the weather was mild. Average morning temps were high teens to low twenties. Well-dressed, or so I thought, I was wearing insulated boot-foot waders that felt warm enough. The upper portion of the waders was thin rubber, a canvas-like material. Layering underneath seemed to make up for the thin waders. Come mid-December, temps plunged below zero. I got excited because I knew the colder and nastier it got, the more birds flew. I admit, though, that after getting my waders wet on a ten-below morning and watching a sheet of ice cover them, a degree of uncertainty crept in. The waders became stiffer to move around in. But things seemed fine for the moment. I thought nothing of the continuous groaning and crunching sound the ice-encased waders made.

The hunt was good, producing three greenheads and one common goldeneye, my first of that species. The temperature warmed up maybe a degree. Water droplets splashed onto my gun barrel and froze as I waded out to pick up decoys. My waders creaked yet again, and new wrinkles formed in the ice sheet covering them. Slinging my 870, I loaded up dekes to head in and trudged across several braids of river channel. Moving along, my left foot felt different from my right: a little wet, a little numb. At first glance, everything appeared normal: no holes in the waders that I could see. The numbness became more pronounced as I neared the I-90 bridge. A closer look revealed long, slender cracks up and down the left leg of the waders.

Back at the truck, I got the heater going and turned all air flow to the floor vents. The waders were frozen so stiff they stood up on their own once I got out of them. My left foot was soaked. If not for layering up, wool socks and the insulated boot foot, the situation could have been much worse. My toes were numb. I got in the truck and massaged them to get the blood flowing while holding them under the heater vent. I felt sure they would resume feeling normal as the cab warmed up. My foot warmed a little, from numb to more of a tingle. Once home, I ran a hot bath and soaked for a bit. My big toe didn't feel quite right for a while after that. I'm pretty sure I had the beginnings of frostbite. I should consider myself lucky I didn't go down in the river and fill up my waders.

I got a better pair of waders the next season: 5mm neoprene overlaid with cordura and a boot foot with 1200-gram Thinsulate. I felt unstoppable. When the subzero stuff hit, I got after it, and though I had a sheet of ice covering the outside of the waders, it just cracked off as I walked. I stayed warm and dry on the inside. Of course, several years of this will take its toll on anything, and the waders eventually leaked—but not before I got several seasons' worth of use out of them. Luckily for me, the leak was small enough and the waders thick enough that I didn't notice it until I got home. One weakness in these waders I have found is in the boot. A necessary evil of hunting just about anywhere can be fence crossings. In Montana, this means barbed wire. Don't use your wader's boot foot to hold down the bottom strand. In my case, it created the tiniest of holes I didn't find out about until it was too late. I tried everything I could to repair it, from filling the hole with silicone to melting it shut with a soldering iron. But the boot just flexes too much for that stuff to stay put. Another problem is that once the Thinsulate inside the boot is penetrated with moisture, it is near impossible to dry out, as it is encased in rubber. Even boot driers can't seem to get the job done.

A fact of where I live that lends itself to good cold-weather duck hunting is the abundance of warm springs that flow into area streams. Find these places, and on the right days, you'll have shooting so good it feels criminal. Many of these spots are on private land requiring access permission. Others you can get to under the auspices of Montana's stream access law. A handful can be found on public land, too. I've hunted such water all three ways and

Spring creeks hold ducks in good numbers below zero.

shot limits on public and private ground. Early on, I was relegated to public access only, but the longer I lived in the Three Forks area, the more I got to know a few landowners gracious enough to give me access. This takes time and is a lot harder now than it used to be.

One special place I call Bob's Slough. You won't find it on any maps, as this isn't its official name, but I call it that because the slough sits on a ranch owned by my friend Bob, a local cattleman and fellow hunter education instructor. Bob's place isn't a secret, and getting permission to hunt there can be a bit like setting up a tee time (I'm not a golfer, but I know a few). Bob is particular about who he lets hunt down there, and I don't blame him. He's had more than a few entitlement-mentality trespassers on his place. If you tell him it's just you hunting, it'd better be just you. If he gives you a certain spot to hunt, you'd better hunt that spot and nowhere else. And the hunting is good.

The first time Mom ever went on a duck hunt with me was here. She was up for a visit between Christmas and New Year's, and we got the good stuff in terms of weather: a tad below zero. A light snow came with it. The morning of the hunt was clear and calm with no wind. Bob had built a hard-sided blind several years ago, which helped with the warmth. I added my portable propane heater to keep Roxy thawed out and the blind comfy. I also set Mom up in my minus-forty-rated sleeping bag. Topping it off with a thermos of fresh coffee, we were set.

The stars twinkled bright on our short walk to the blind. As we settled in, the horizon came alive with the brilliant colors of dawn. With daylight, the air filled with the sound of whistling pintails circling above. I pointed out the drake's distinct tail feathers to Mom. The long sprigs stood out on their dark forms in the still, dim light. At shooting time, I shot a drake pintail that fell onto the ice across the slough from us. I decided that was the one pintail I wanted to shoot today and the rest would be mallards. For the first twenty minutes, all that flew were pintails. Then greenheads started showing up. They came in small groups of three to four birds at a time. The bright sunlight made their breeding plumage shimmer. After shooting a couple, close inspection revealed they were in prime shape for eating, with a nice layer of orange fat.

A darker bird dropped in, and at quick glance, I judged it a gadwall drake. Hoping to have a good mix in the bag, I made a clean kill only to confirm it was in fact a pintail hen. Bad call: at the time, there was a two-bird limit on pintails. It provided a good opportunity for Mom to see a male/female pair up close, though. Both of us would eat well. Roxy was having a good time of it. With steady flights, retrieves came at regular intervals, and she was in full form. Her eyes stayed locked on the sky. Mom marveled at her intensity and enthusiasm when birds fell from the sky.

At one point, I had to step out to answer the call. I was standing in willows near the edge of the slough, shotgun in the blind, when a flight of nine mallards dropped into the slough feet from the bank, right in front of us. Doing my best, I tried to ease back into the blind. Of course, the birds high-tailed it at my first step. I told Mom that she'd seen a classic duck-hunting moment. Get out of arm's reach of your gun, and they will come.

In the shooting lull that followed, a pair of trumpeter swans glided in, landing with apt smoothness. The landing was preceded by their awkward-sounding call that doesn't match up with their graceful appearance. Another first for Mom. Right around the time the swans were swimming serenely across the slough, a kingfisher perched on a willow branch right outside the blind. Mom's day was made. For a birder, it doesn't get much better.

By eleven thirty, I'd collected a limit: five mallard, two pintail. The temperature had warmed a few degrees but was still below ten degrees. Of all the hunts Mom could have witnessed in my duck-hunting life, I couldn't have scripted this one better. I was also grateful it was a comfortable experience for her, given the conditions and how uncomfortable many of my previous hunts had been. Mom enjoyed herself and said she now understood why I duck hunted. Not that she ever questioned my reasons, but words can't beat firsthand experience.

Several Thanksgiving Days ago, I had a lot to be thankful for as I sat back waiting for the ducks to come in. Hunting season had been good to me. Elk and deer were in the freezer: the real chore of hunting season was done. Roxy and I had already had some good days afield in early October. I'd shot my first limit of pheasant over her, too. Life was good. Basking in the glow of warm autumn memories, I kept my eyes on the frigid horizon. Roxy did the same. It was a good day to be hunting ducks over a warm spring on a subzero morning.

Thanksgiving can be a warmer-than-average time here, but it wasn't that year. At five below, it was colder than expected. Roxy and I didn't need anyone to tell us what to do that morning. As we walked into our spot, ducks flushed off the spring-fed puddles. The dense, chill air cracked with quacks and whistles. I put out a small spread of eleven dekes, five on a jerk string and one flapper. Tucking into the cattails, I loaded up my Browning Gold semiauto and watched dawn break over the east rim of the valley.

Attack of the mallards. *Roger Parker.*

I only watch 180 degrees of the horizon in front of me. Roxy has everything else. All I do is watch her eyes and ears. If ducks are specks on the horizon, she is locked onto them. I know to get ready, maybe at most put my drake call to my lips. That's how it went at shooting time that morning. I heard the air rush as they cupped. We held tight until they pitched in, and I scored a double. Roxy fetched them up in short order: greenheads, and they looked to be putting on weight.

Pouring hot coffee from the thermos, I sipped it with utter contentment. I couldn't enjoy it long, though, as more birds were on the move now. I didn't have to do too much high-balling that morning. This was probably the first time ducks had been frozen out that season, so they weren't super wary like they would be in January. Three more greenheads fell over the dekes with some dispersed mallard calls. I wouldn't say the ducks were pouring in that morning, but they came in steady.

With five in the bag, I got a little giddy: a limit might be in the cards today. Not two minutes later, a bunch of green-winged teal bombed into the hole, and I scored a double. Thanksgiving limit! The day was bright and sunny, the air cold and clear, with no wind. The weather was the icing on the cake on top of a limit. Loading gear, dekes and ducks into the sled and dragging it back to the truck, Roxy at my side in her neoprene vest, I thanked God about fifty times. It just doesn't get any better. It was, indeed, a day to be thankful for.

It's hard to say what gets a duck hunter excited in midlife. I think it's a little different for each of us. The dog, for sure: she's the only reason I feel right going when I don't want to. Seeing the temp below zero on the thermometer does it, too. With the right water, you know it's gonna be good.

CHAPTER 4

GOOD MEDICINE

"Good Medicine" was originally published in the Fall 2021 issue of Strung: A Sporting Journal.

Fall is a coveted time, more so with each passing year. Its gentle, warm, angular light soothes in ways we feel but can't fully know. The feeling of impending transition is ever present as each day wanes by the minute, intimating glimpses of your own autumn. You realize there's maybe more time behind you than in front. Wasting an ounce of it seems criminal. Even the pessimist in us seeks what is good about life this time of year and soaks up every drop there is.

Medicine Lake National Wildlife Refuge sits in the far northeast corner of Montana (North Dakota is literally minutes away, depending on how fast you drive). It's in the middle of the Prairie Pothole Region, which has produced much of the continent's waterfowl for centuries. People are scarce in these parts. Not far across the state line lies the confluence of the Missouri and Yellowstone Rivers. The refuge and surrounding area don't see much traffic until about the second weekend of October. Along with being prime waterfowl habitat, this is the beginning of the pheasant breadbasket that stretches into the Dakotas.

This destination had been on my to-do list, with no plans to go anytime soon. They say there's no better time than right now. But this isn't a place you go to on a whim. By the time I got home, I knew, an additional thousand miles would be on the odometer—that's without leaving the state. A photograph did it. I was in Missoula for work, sitting in a hotel room, when the photo came through in a text from my friend Wade Hill. Wade, his brother Sean and Jamie Young make an annual pilgrimage out there for the pheasant opener. Wade had been putting the pressure on that I should join them this year. I came up with a million excuses as to why I couldn't. Then I opened the text. Sean had gone up ahead of everybody to stake their claim on a small piece of public ground near the refuge. He'd been out scouting and sending back reports.

I saw a photo of ducks winging their way across a prairie pond among fall shades of green and tan, bathed in brilliant sunlight. Nothing out here escapes the sun's touch with so little to break it up: no mountains, no trees, just wide-open rolling prairie. The ducks looked like mallard, maybe gadwall. I thought of Roxy and her gray chin whiskers. Opening weekend of duck season had been less than productive. The sight of those mallards in the prairie sunlight of late afternoon struck a chord deep within me. In less than ten minutes, I talked to the wife, emailed a vacation request to the boss and let Wade know I was in. Mentally, I was already there. Two days later, Roxy and I were loaded in the truck heading east.

We set off straight from work about three o'clock with a vault of music and audiobooks and a thermos of coffee to make the 460-mile trek east. When we pulled into camp a little before midnight, Wade and Jamie were still up. They came walking out of the horse trailer that doubled as a cook shack. Wade handed me a cold beer. They'd been taking in the pleasant prairie night; everyone else had turned in. They gave me the rundown. Wake-up was four-thirty. Wade's dad, Larry, would have breakfast going. At five-thirty, we'd roll out to a block management area down the road and stake a claim with our four trucks. Any hunter in his right mind would keep driving.

Roxy and I settled in for a few hours of sleep. You can see dawn coming for a long ways out here. It's a long line of light infinitely spanning the horizon that is visible more than an hour before sunrise. Spirits were high as we stood around the trucks at the ranch sign-in box. Wade, Jamie and the rest of the crew had hunted this place the last several years running. As we sipped coffee in the mildly cool air, the sound of a rooster pheasant echoed among the Russian olive shelterbelts. We were minutes from stepping off to walk them.

There were nine of us hunting that morning: me; Wade; his wife, Nicki; Jamie; his wife, Rae Lynn; Sean; Medora and Lindsay, two younger family friends and both new hunters; and finally, Jim and Joe, doctors from the Bozeman area who worked with Nicki and Rae Lynn, both nurses. We had medical emergencies covered. The air of anticipation was palpable on the canine scene, too. I had Roxy. There were Wade and Nicki's two

Brittanys, Ohms and Tess. Then Argus, Sean's drahthaar. Jim and Joe had another Brittany and a black Lab pup. Shooting time upon us, we staged at the head of our respective shelterbelts. Me, Roxy, Jamie and Rae Lynn took off together. Roosters were crowing feet away as we stepped off. Roxy got birdy out of the gate, her nose leading her into the shelterbelt. Wings fluttered among the Russian olives. Pheasants flushed from multiple directions, and shotguns thumped across the prairie. The first two birds in front of me were hens. Then a long-tailed rooster flushed. I folded him on the first shot from my Citori. Roxy fetched him up, hard-mouthing him a bit before bringing him in.

Shotguns continued thumping in all directions as birds took off in disarray and confusion. I bagged a second rooster. The heft in my game vest felt good. The smarter birds were staying in the shelterbelts and running to the far end. What often happens is that they will bunch up at the end of the belt. When the hunters get there, a mass flushing of birds happens. At the end of these belts was a long irrigation ditch lined with tall grass and cattails. The pheasants piled into this stuff. Walking the next shelterbelt over, back on the road, we met up with Jim and Joe, who had the water bowls out getting their dogs hydrated. Roxy sidled up next to them for a drink. We talked while the dogs got their fill, their legs wobbly and noses overwhelmed with bird scent.

Roxy, head up now, lifted her nose toward a clump of grass maybe twenty yards away. She moseyed casually over to it. When she poked her head into the grass, a rooster flushed a foot from her head. We headed back to the nearest shelterbelt, walking both sides. Some hens flushed but no roosters. Roxy was starting to look a little tuckered, her stamina shorter with age. I figured it was probably time for us to head toward the truck. Rae Lynn and I were walking opposite sides of an irrigation ditch. Roxy went down into it. As she did, several roosters got up. Rae Lynn scored a double, and I dropped one on my second shot, the two of us limited out. Jamie, right behind us, couldn't shoot. It was eight fifteen in the morning.

The prairie sprawled to the horizon in all directions. Isolated stands of cottonwood popped gold intermittently, leaves gently shaking in the breeze that had been picking up since midmorning. With the day ahead of us, Roxy and I went scouting for ducks. Nearing the refuge, I could see faint slivers of blue cutting open the tan prairie. Bulrush and cattail lined the water's edge. We'd arrived at Medicine Lake. I picked up a map from the kiosk. The place is big. Scouting it effectively requires a vehicle and binoculars. An initial canvas of the water did not reveal large numbers of

Author and Roxy with limit of ring-necked pheasant, northeast Montana. *Rae Lynn Young.*

ducks. Not far in, I crossed paths with the refuge warden. He confirmed what I saw: the ducks just weren't here yet and this was a slow year in terms of the fall flight's arrival. He recommended checking out the smaller ponds east of the main lake as well as the waterfowl production areas (WPAs) northeast of the refuge.

We drove toward Swanson Lake. Pulling up, I could see a few scattered rafts of ducks on the far end of the pond. Rooster pheasants crowed in the bulrushes and cattails as we approached the lakeshore. Just short of the lake, I spotted a small boulder with a plaque on it. I walked up to read the plaque: "Swanson Lake. Dedicated to the memory of Shannon Swanson, 1963–2007. Husband, friend, naturalist, wildland firefighter. We will always remember your quick wit, easy smile, contagious laugh, and optimistic outlook on life." I paused after reading and took in the lake and its surroundings while Roxy probed the grass beyond in a zigzag fashion, nose to the wind. It was apparent that Shannon spent a lot of time here, touched people's hearts and loved life. Etched on the plaque was a hunter gazing skyward at ducks, shotgun resting on his right shoulder and a brace of ducks in his left hand. Clearly, this place was special to him. I can relate. Most times, the good medicine we need doesn't come from a pharmacy.

Roxy and I walked the shoreline, jumping a couple of pheasant in the process. Obviously, numbers were doing well, and it was clear any duck-hunting efforts here would certainly hold the possibility of roosters. Driving to the north side of the refuge, I made note of other potholes, but it was clear Swanson was where we needed to be. The ducks were there.

The effect of just four hours' sleep and the long drive from Three Forks was now sinking in. I pointed the truck back south. Lunch and a nap were in order. Back in camp, hunters were stretched out in camp chairs, soaking in the noonday sun. The day's pheasants were lined up, hanging from a single strand of barbed wire on a fence line. Nicki and Rae Lynn were working on dressing the birds with a dinner plan for this evening. Wade and Jamie's kids ran through the grass and rode bikes up and down the dirt two-track, having the time of their lives. Roxy and I found some shade next to the truck and lay down for a much-needed rest. Midday naps in camp are a critical staple of the sporting life. I don't recommend forgoing them.

I awoke about four thirty feeling refreshed in the clean prairie air. Everybody was stirring and moving about. It sounded like we had a plan developing for an evening walk to help Medora get her limit. She was the only hunter in camp who hadn't gotten one today. The rest of us would take advantage of any sharptails we came upon. Wade, leaving his shotgun in camp, shouldered his Canon DSLR. Nicki got Tess ready to go. Ohms stayed in camp to give Tess more points. Roxy hung back in camp to rest her aging hips. The public ground we were camped on had ample cover, and roosters could be heard not far from camp. Tess, out front, went on point with camp in sight. A hen flushed to our left, straight up and over our heads.

"Hen!" Nicki hollered out.

A few guns went up, but nobody shot. We'd barely stepped off before Tess went on point again.

"Rooster!" Nicki's voice echoed down the line.

The rooster got up, its long tail wobbling like a whip antenna. Unfortunately, it was too far out of Medora's swing to get a shot. Those were the only two birds we flushed. We casually walked back toward camp. On our way back, we noticed something out of place on the skyline: a large, dark form consistent with the size of a horse or a cow. It was neither. In my mind, I knew exactly what it was, but our feet being on the high prairie caused me to doubt.

"Wade, look over there. I think we got us a moose!" I could now make out a small set of antlers.

Indeed it was. Wade's shutter clicked as he focused in on the out-of-place cervid. It seemed unusual to us, but it's not so out there these days. A recent trend has been moose migrating back and forth from southern Saskatchewan into northeast Montana. Medicine Lake provides some good habitat for them, too. It was an odd but memorable way to finish off our evening walk.

In camp, the mood was light as we kicked back while Nicki walked around offering up barbecued pheasant morsels bathed in a tangy mustard sauce. Meanwhile, Larry was in the horse trailer grilling up New York strips to order: nothing too good for this bird camp. While everyone else was talking of pheasant, Jamie and I were quietly having a conversation about duck-hunting prospects for tomorrow. While I had soaked up every ounce of this day, thoughts of Medicine Lake's shoreline and her ducks kept intruding on the present moment. We agreed that Swanson Lake was our best option. Wade concurred.

Dusk came on, the prairie sun well below the western horizon. Our focus shifted north. As dark settled in, the aurora came out where the prairie met the sky. With a fresh belt of single malt in my tin cup, I stared at the undulating light show, stroking Roxy's head rested on my knee. A moment of silence overtook the camp as this miracle of nature performed. For the blessings we had this day, what could be better than to see this at the end of it?

Of course, I'd looked at the wrong sunrise/sunset table before turning in. Montana requires four of them, as it takes daylight a little bit to filter across the fourth-largest state. Naturally tired, combined with the effect of two good belts of Glenfiddich fifteen-year, I went right to the time zone covering my home range. Luckily it all worked out—and when it comes to legal shooting time, better late than early. We set up a little after shooting time, and nobody complained or seemed upset that we'd started off late. It had been a later night for some than for others. So we pitched decoys out in broad daylight.

Joining me in the blind that morning were Wade, Sean, Medora and Lindsay. Jamie said he would join me for the afternoon hunt. Dark clouds hung over us that morning, with rain and high winds forecast after midmorning. The birds that did fly were well out of range on the opposite shoreline. The rest were rafted up in a far corner. A single flew by, and I took the only shot, hitting well behind it. I watched my lonely wad disappear below the skyline.

Pheasants could be heard crowing in the cattails. I told the crew to feel free to go see about the pheasants as I didn't think the morning would get any better. It didn't take any pushing, and they were off. I was content to sit in the blind a bit longer with Roxy, taking in the expanse of the prairie and

Medicine Lake National Wildlife Refuge at dawn, northeast Montana.

Swanson Lake. Hunting here in solitude seemed more appropriate, anyway. While we sat there watching the empty sky, Roxy slowly began to walk toward the lake's edge. Not thinking much of it, I urged her back. She stayed where she was, eyes fixed toward the bank. I stood up to go grab her and saw the tail feathers of a rooster pheasant bounding off into the bulrushes and cattails. That bird had walked up within feet of us sitting there!

About four o'clock in the afternoon, Jamie and I loaded up for the evening duck hunt. Roxy was rested. The skies were clearing to the west as the wind buffeted the prairie. Arriving at the lake, we settled on a narrow channel that flowed between Swanson and Medicine Lakes. Here we had grass tall enough for cover as well as a windbreak. It was also less likely we'd lose birds to the wind here. Backs to the sun, we pitched out a hasty spread and hunkered into the cattail lining the ditch.

Not long into it, we got pass shots at blue-winged teal, which hit well behind, unable to connect through the gale. Then a moment came—one of those moments that lasts only a few seconds but is what you came there for. It's the moment you must do everything right, as it's the culminating event of the trip. It's an epic moment, even though you don't know it at the time.

Jamie and I were hunkered down from the wind. It was still early season, so I had Roxy on a lead to keep her from jumping the shot, as she was prone to do until at least the third or fourth hunt of the year. But she'd been doing well, so I unclipped the lead. The evening sun was sitting low and casting a brilliant light across the water and tawny grass. To the southeast, the crescendo of thousands of sandhill cranes' primordial staccato echoed across the land, an eerie sound. The prehistoric murmuration stretched across the sky, staging for migration south.

Then came the moment, as if the sandhill scene wasn't enough. A lone drake canvasback buzzed in at deck level from nowhere, maybe two feet off the water.

"Canvasback! Shoot him!" Jamie shouted.

His burgundy-shaded head, black breast collar, white body and gray-tipped wings couldn't have looked more brilliant in the setting sun. He was everything you'd look for in a wall specimen, and he was the first one I'd ever seen up close, maybe even too close to shoot. I raised my shotgun at a range I couldn't miss. At that moment, Roxy was up and running, smack dab between me and the bird. I'd have taken her head off had I shot. I lowered my gun and cursed her, even though it was me who unclipped her lead earlier.

Jamie and I watched the lone drake, in his fall splendor, sail out over the lake, disappearing into the creeping dusk. Oh, how I wanted that bird. That one bird. He might as well have been a bighorn ram disappearing over the next ridgeline, the way I felt about it. By now, it was sunset and time to pick up the dekes. Jamie looked over at me with a slight grin.

"You'll never have that happen again!" He could have meant a couple of things. "You'll never let that dog loose again," or "You'll never see another drake canvasback that close."

We picked up our decoys as the sun sank below the western horizon. The sandhills' staccato echoed past dusk. Walking away, not a duck to hand, I don't think I spent one second thinking about that fact—just about the canvasback and the scene that had surrounded us all evening. Some hunts are meant to only whet the appetite for more. This was beginning to be one of them. Driving back to camp, Jamie talked of a November trip. He said that was when it could really be good here. Perhaps.

The next morning, I snuck out of camp before dawn, alone, back to Swanson Lake. Just me and Roxy. We set up on the opposite shoreline. The wind had gone. A gentle, partly cloudy day was coming in. I managed to score on a gadwall and a hen ruddy. By the time we were picking up, the prairie was bathed in a gentle October morning glow. Back on the tailgate, shimmying out of my waders, I took a good look around.

Timing is everything in life. Sometimes you just throw caution to the wind and dive in. Two years later, a pheasant rooster's crow couldn't be heard within a hundred miles of here. Hard winters the likes of which we hadn't seen for probably twenty years decimated their numbers. In that same time, I lost Roxy. If you wait for things to be perfect, you'll never get anything done that's worth doing. One of the best moves I've made on a whim, it made me wish I had done so more often.

CHAPTER 5

NO KING'S RIVER, NOBODY'S SEWER

I t was a cold, hard morning. The front had pushed through a couple of days before. The mercury plummeted to the subzero realm. Snow was still falling. The main river channel creaked and groaned, transitioning into an ice field. In the early morning hours, Banded Creek called my name. I'd taken up a new challenge and purchased an old twelve-gauge side by side. I'd been reading Don Thomas and Worth Mathewson. If you don't get the urge to try a double from these guys, you're not enjoying the reading enough. I also packed a dozen rubber collapsible Deek-brand decoys. Both brought an air of nostalgia, challenge and efficiency to my process.

The double was not fancy or expensive. The kind of hunting I did could be hard on stuff. There's a reason shotguns marketed to duck hunters favor composite-stocked repeating actions. However, nothing beats the look and feel of an old double in your hands, going about your business as your great-grandfather might have done. The gun was a Kirk twelve-gauge with double triggers. Never heard of Kirk shotguns? Neither had I. This would have been one you found in the pages of a Sears, Roebuck catalog back in the day. I picked it up for around $300 at Capitol Sports in Helena.

Stepping off onto the ice-choked Madison, I made my way in the predawn darkness to Banded Creek. The snow-covered landscape created so much light, I didn't need a headlamp. Coming up the main channel just short of the creek, I spotted three nicely furred-up coyotes loping across the ice. Such conditions expanded their prowling range significantly. I stopped to watch them in the predawn gloom as light flurries swirled about. Turning up the creek, I was dismayed to find an unusually thick amount of slush flowing into it from the ice-gorged Madison. This freeze-up had come so quick and so fast that the mouth of the creek was solid ice and the water level was significantly higher than usual, making it too deep for mallards to fancy. It wasn't much fun for me, either. Too late now: I was here and not sure how well I would fare.

Once I got to a spot along the creek that wasn't full of slush yet and relatively shallow, I threw out a hasty deke spread and slipped two no. 4s in the double. The sound and feel of a double locking shut is one of many reasons to hunt with one. It's a sweet, old sound, in the same category as the steel *ping* a quality axe makes when splitting wood. Lightly gripping the double, I watched the sky through the gently falling snow swirling in the light north wind that carried a stiff bite for its speed. A single medium-sized duck came buzzing along the creek a bit high. I shouldered, fired and watched the bird fold stone-dead. Breaking the double, I reloaded the full choke barrel—no ejectors on this baby. Fetching up the bird, I saw it was a drake goldeneye. Not the best eating, but we'd make him work. What goldeneyes lack in taste, they make up for in appearance: a beautiful bird, especially in December.

This was the first time Banded Creek proved a tough option. The nature of the conditions that day was not going to bring in mallards. It goes to show you that five years of stable weather conditions do nothing more than lull you into a false sense of security. This winter was shaping up to be a ten-year event. According to longtime Three Forks rancher Bob Lane, who was born in the 1930s, hard winters seem to come around every ten years, mostly around the eighth or ninth year of the decade. It was 2008. This had indeed been the coldest, snowiest winter I'd seen since moving to Montana. The last real hard winter had been in '98.

Watching the slush-filled creek flow slower with each minute and with one duck to show for it, I gathered my deeks, stuffed the goldeneye among them and began the walk out. I came around the bend in the creek where it meets the long slough from which the warm spring rises. The snow was blowing sideways. The creek was frozen over, and I was walking on ice. About fifty yards away, I saw two pickups parked next to the slough. Two hunters were loading up decoys. One saw me, and I waved back. At my wave, he came walking over in a hurry.

"What are you doing here!?" the landowner said in an angry tone.

"Keeping between the high-water marks," I said, to reiterate a key tenant of the stream access law.

Banded Creek bounty.

"You trespassed to get here!" he said. "I'll call Joe right now, and we'll get him to settle this!"

Joe was the local game warden sergeant. I knew Joe myself. I'd just spent time in the field with him working on an article about Montana wardens. We'd discussed this very subject, and I had a fairly good idea how he'd handle it. At the time, I was eight years out from being a game warden but working as a police officer, and I had enough experience to know this guy was trying to intimidate me, plain and simple. He was not a fan of the stream access law. Anything he was trying to stop me from doing was a moot point now, as my hunt was over and I was headed back along the river legally. Being a weekday, I figured it was probably Joe's day off. The last thing I wanted was for him to have to come out here in this weather and waste his time.

"Sir, I've been below the high-water marks the whole time," I replied.

"You've been trespassing all over the place! Look, my wife's an attorney, and you don't want to argue the stream access law with me," he said.

"Sir, I was not trespassing. I'm going to leave now," I replied.

"Y-yes," he stammered. "I'd like you to leave."

I continued toward the main river channel, then began my walk back along the channel to my parking spot. I was maybe fifty yards upriver when his truck pulled up atop the bank. *Great*, I thought. *What does he want now?*

"Where did you come in from?" he asked.

"From the fishing access. You can see my truck parked over there." I pointed in the direction of my truck.

The guy hung his head, hands on hips.

"Look, I'm sorry I blew up back there. I've had a lot of problems with people poaching deer on my place and vandalizing my deer stands. I really respect you for being out on a day like today. It's pretty miserable to be out in this. Between you and me, yeah, that channel is part of the river, even though it's not navigable. I'll admit it's a gray area. The stream access law has a lot of gray area."

Our conversation continued as the snow blew sideways. I expressed appreciation for his eventual understanding. He went on to tell me about his pheasant release program and how birds don't just hang out on his property. He told me how he owns the islands in the river but doesn't care or worry if people hunt on them. I told him his conservation efforts and generosity were appreciated and that people committing criminal acts on his property was not OK. He nodded in thanks.

By now, we were both wondering. As the conversation progressed, it was clear two southerners were talking.

"Where you from?" he asked.

"Louisiana."

"Atlanta. Name's Greg."

"Matt."

This was the first stream access conflict I ever experienced. It taught me a few things from a hunter behavior standpoint. First, actions speak louder than words. Once Greg realized the lengths I had gone to get to where I was legally, he realized he was in the wrong or at least had doubts about his actions. Being a duck hunter himself, he expressed mutual respect because I was doing it right under tough conditions. The second lesson, and this one is most important: being calm and deferring to the other party may be hard, but it can defuse an escalated situation where there are firearms present. You maintain the upper hand when you do this. Be tactful and don't let pride get in the way. It's never worth going beyond a verbal altercation unless self-defense is involved. Be a good witness and contact the authorities as soon as possible to communicate your side of events. There are always two sides to a story.

That was the last time I ever hunted Banded Creek. Oh, sure, I could have gone back. However, it was clear that conflict surrounding the spot was on the rise. Knowing there were possibly violations occurring in the area, I didn't want to be associated with any of it. My main reason for hunting here was to relax and unwind. I didn't want to feel like I had to be looking over my shoulder every time I went back. It would just ruin it. Besides, I felt I'd gotten the best of what it had to offer anyway. There had also been a gradual increase in hunting pressure in the area, which would only exacerbate tensions between landowners and public hunters. I wanted no part in that. With overcrowding and legitimate trespass violations on the rise in the years since, even the islands in the river, which are private land, are now posted. I can't say I wouldn't do the same thing if I owned the land.

One of the things that makes Montana so friendly to the average sportsman is its stream access law. This law, established in 1972 and upheld in 1984 by the state supreme court, allows anyone to access rivers and streams at bridges on public roads, fishing access sites, state parks and other public access points. Access to these waters is granted for the purpose of water-based recreation: think fishing, waterfowl hunting, floating, etc. Once you're on stream, you must stay below the ordinary high-water marks. Basically, beneath your feet must be what would normally be underwater in an ordinary year's spring runoff. Think gravel, not hard-packed dry dirt. A

Montana's stream access law opens up a world of opportunity for duck hunters.

person is allowed under the law to go above the high-water marks in order to bypass man-made obstacles or hazards: think a barbed wire fence you can't safely float underneath or a steep bank of riprap that would be hazardous to traverse. You must go around such hazards in the least intrusive manner possible. Big-game hunting or trapping between the ordinary high-water marks is not allowed. Walking the riverbank through private to public land to hunt big game or trap is not allowed. However, floating through private to public land where you would big game hunt or trap is OK: hence "water-based activity."[*]

Many landowners are fine with the stream access law, many indifferent, some downright hostile toward it. This law has had its constitutionality challenged numerous times in both state and federal court.[†] Some of the country's wealthiest have tried taking on this law with the intent of having it overturned. All have met with failure. As Montana's population increases and more stream users take advantage of the opportunity, there are likely to be more challenges. While I firmly believe in the stream access law, I also believe in respecting private property rights. As with any contentious issue, there are two sides, and neither is without sin. Public access to recreational opportunities is beneficial to the common good. Any community is better off when everyone has a place to recreate outdoors. It's safe to say that I would not have experienced such a rich variety of hunting and angling experiences were it not for the Montana Stream Access Law.

At the same time, abuses have created conflict where it could have been avoided. True, some landowners simply don't want anyone using streams that flow through their land and believe they own the water, too. A lot of landowners have no strong feelings for or against the stream access law. Maybe they even like seeing an occasional angler or duck hunter pass by. Then happens along a hunter either ignorant of the law or intent on doing whatever he pleases. In Montana, hunting without landowner permission is illegal, and it is the hunter's responsibility to know where they are at all times, posted signs or not. Add to that the GPS capabilities hunters have available today to determine their exact location and who owns the ground they're standing on, and nobody has excuses for trespassing in ignorance anymore. Montana state law stipulates it is the hunter's, not the landowner's, responsibility to know if they have permission to hunt somewhere or not. Still, there are those who will do it no matter what, and they will use stream

---

[*] Montana State Legislature, *Montana Code Annotated 2023*.
[†] Lane, "Remarkable Odyssey," 168.

access as a starting point to commit their crimes. Most people try to do the right thing, but the few who don't earn everybody on the water a reputation they don't deserve.

Then there is the time of year duck hunters aren't even around—but they get lumped in with other peoples' bad behavior come fall. Enter Memorial Day, Fourth of July and Labor Day. On these holidays and nearly every weekend in between, there can be hundreds, in some cases thousands, of people getting on the river to float, maybe fish, but mostly drink and do other things. The landowner may choose not to look at the river on that particular day. But come Monday morning, he decides to go down for a peaceful walk along the riverbank and finds himself traversing a minefield of glass bottles, beer cans, hypodermic needles, lost flip-flops and other detritus of recreational floating, often scattered over several river miles. It is only getting worse the more people move here. Then there is the Sunday afternoon knock on the door by the deputy sheriff and an ambulance crew to request access through their property to the river to respond to a medical emergency. Maybe it's alcohol poisoning, a drug overdose. Maybe someone decided to climb a thirty-foot cliff and jump into the river, only to find it wasn't deep enough to avoid breaking bones. It doesn't take long for the landowner to equate public access with public nuisance.

Incidentally, one local landowner dynamited his thirty-foot cliff a few years back. It reduced the spike of floaters for a little while, but stream traffic has picked back up again. In the last several years, which have seen a real uptick in stream use, I have also seen an exponential increase in the amount of litter. No, it is not my imagination. This is happening. It's not unusual for me to haul a load of trash home from the river after a day of work or play. I shudder to think how much human waste enters the river on a busy summer day during what's locally called the rubber "hatch," which refers to the hordes of recreational floaters on rubber inner tubes. In my neighborhood, the Madison gets the most traffic, but the Jefferson sees its fair share. While the busiest stretch of the Madison is almost all bordered by public land, the Jeff flows mostly through private. Most problems come from recreationists who oftentimes have never heard of the stream access law and for years didn't pay anything into the system to maintain access sites. Historically, hunter and angler dollars paid for fishing access sites and wildlife management areas, not to mention other public access opportunities. Fortunately, recent legislation now requires any recreationist entering a state-owned fishing access site, a wildlife management area or state land to purchase a conservation license. It is hoped this will help shoulder the burden this recreationist group places on

A good early season bag on a drizzly Jefferson River morning.

the resource. It is this kind of activity that burns out landowners on stream access by the time fall hunting seasons roll around.

Full context is important before engaging in a fight over stream access. It's a worthy fight, but the water can get dirty. It is critical that hunters and anglers not only champion access rights but also speak out against access abuses and report violations when they see them. The law won't get them all, but a few is better than nothing. Policing ourselves is probably the best thing we can do. At some point, too, the non-hunting and non-fishing crowd that uses Montana's streams is going to have to get organized and help clean some of this mess up. I will tip my hat to the user groups that have begun organizing end-of-summer cleanup days on the Madison. It's a shame we even have to have such a thing, but it is better than nothing.

One year, Alex Betz and I decided to float hunt the Madison in early October. Indian summer had settled in for who knew how long. This weather doesn't get birds moving around much, but it is heaven to hunt in. If your morning setup over decoys doesn't fill the bag, you can usually eke out a limit with some residual jump shooting on the float out. Things started off in typical fashion for us. We had three dogs in the boat: Roxy,

Duke and Sadie. Sadie, an adopted Lab mix, was of no use, but Alex couldn't leave her at home because she'd destroy the furniture. We were in Alex's johnboat, which sported a homemade camo paint job along with his custom boat blind. He had a paddle and a trolling motor to get us downriver. That lasted approximately five minutes before a chance meeting with a small boulder promptly snapped the trolling motor shaft in two. We had yet to get to our hunting spot.

The plan was to hunt a gravel bar just above a side channel confluence. Here, a nice slick of shallow frog water usually held birds. There was an old cabin nearby on the bank. In all the years I'd hunted the area, I'd never seen anyone using it or any sign that it was occupied. My guess was it belonged to an absentee landowner who flew south come fall. We may have been a few minutes late, but we set up anyway and settled into the beautiful fall morning. The cottonwoods shimmered gold. The willow and red osier dogwood had shed their leaves.

We managed to coax in some birds near our spread. Alex fired at two passing mallards and missed. Not too long after, on the south side of the river, a truck pulled up, and a landowner came out of the brush hollering and screaming at us about shooting too close to somebody else's house. A few things to mention here: (1) We were not shooting at anyone's house. The nearest and only house belonged to, best I could tell over the years, an absentee landowner who was only there in the summer. So it was unoccupied that day, as it usually was that time of year. (2) The gentleman upset with us was engaged in agricultural work, underscoring the rural setting we were in. (3) There is no Montana law stating how close you can or can't shoot near a house, occupied or unoccupied, other than within city limits or on state land. We were well outside of those constraints. (4) Bottom line: we were within our legal right to be where we were and would not have hunted there if it were a safety concern.

We didn't argue with him and kept about our business. He got back in his truck and on the phone, probably calling the game warden or the sheriff. Ten minutes later, he got back out and approached the stream bank. Pointing his finger in the air, he yelled, "It might be legal! But is it right?!"

He promptly got back in his pickup and drove off. Alex and I hung out for a few more minutes and decided we'd missed the good morning action anyway. Best get to jump shooting and get some birds, the way this day was going. The rest of the float went by without incident in terms of conflict or dead ducks. Just above the take-out, we managed to put the sneak on some mallards, and I dropped one. All of that for one duck! We easily could have

A duck hunter walks below the high-water mark.

let our late start or tiff with the landowner dampen the mood. All we could do was laugh about it. Alex must have uttered that landowner's final words ten times the rest of the float. Still, you couldn't beat the weather, and the fall colors were reason enough to float the river that day.

It might be legal, but is it right?

You can argue right and wrong about everything all day long. What I can say about Montana's stream access law as it applies to everyone is that it is a fundamental good. It must be respected as any privilege should be, and as always, your rights end where another's begin. In this case, it is the ordinary high-water mark.

CHAPTER 6

OF DUCKS AND MOUNTAIN MEN

The Three Forks of the Missouri was a region said to possess a wealth in furs not surpassed by the mines of Peru.
—St. Louis Enquirer, *April 13, 1822*

The burn trail cut the early morning sky as the shooting star plunged into oblivion. The air was crisp, fall perfect. I leaned on the tailgate of my pickup, hands in my wader chest pocket, gazing up at the stars. Kevin Murphy would be here any minute and we'd step off for a new hole on the Madison. Just upriver from the fishing access, the river disperses into a maze of braids and channels among head-high willows and gravel bars in the shadow of the Spanish Peaks. We'd explored it a few days before and found a small slough cut off from the main channel, hidden in a depression among the gravel bars: perfect puddle duck depth. Driftwood and nearby willows provided the makings for a blind. In the process of building it, we spooked a cow moose from her bed.

The primary obstacle that kept most hunters at bay was a swift, waist-deep channel bolstered on one side by a long bank of concrete riprap. You had to be careful climbing down it and stepping off into the stiff current. It only took a few steps to get through the swift stuff and you were fine. We made the crossing in the beam of our headlamps and were on our way. Past the crossing, our energies focused on avoiding a close encounter with a moose in the dark.

All went according to plan, and we were set up over our decoys with ten minutes to spare. Dawn broke before us in crisp hues of orange, pink and blue. The sky backlit cottonwoods lining the bank. We sipped coffee and kept our ears to the wind for the sound of wings and mallard talk. Luckily for us, it was a light wind. Peering out of the blind, I saw four teal on the water. Where they came from, who knows. I whispered to Kevin that we had ducks out front. Our guns came up. The ducks flew up so fast and close, Kevin could have whacked one with his gun barrel. No shots were fired.

While the morning was grand, ducks proved elusive. Perhaps this wasn't the hot spot we'd hoped for. A single passed behind us, a mallard drake. I worked him with my drake call. He came in on Kevin's swing to our left. Kevin folded him with one shot. Not long after that, I folded a mallard hen passing overhead. Things fizzled after that. We were into the doughnuts early. A small flight of birds touched down on a beaver pond upriver. We put on a sneak but not good enough. The birds got airborne well out of range. At that, we picked up the dekes and headed out.

Back at the swift channel crossing, I went first. Kevin would wait until I was up the riprap before going himself. The rock rolled underfoot as I made my first step up. In I went. My army rucksack full of dekes and gear helped send me downstream in a hurry, thanks to the stiff current. The sudden shock of being dunked in the cold water induced deep gasps for air. Inches from the riprap, I scrambled to grab it as my waders filled up. As the scene unfolded, I made movements to scuttle my rucksack and shotgun. Then, as my body came parallel with the riprap, I felt my feet hit bottom, stopping my downstream momentum. My now-numb hands grabbed hold of the rocks. I pulled myself up the bank and got out with all my stuff. If only I could shake off like a Lab.

Kevin, meanwhile, had crossed and was coming my way. The walk to the truck was a short one, and the temp just above freezing. Kevin and I had a laugh over it, then he said, "Finally, someone else going in the water besides me." He was usually the one to fall in and get wet. All that for two ducks! It's staggering, the things men do for fins, feathers and fur. It's an old story, too.

Lewis and Clark arrived at the confluence of the Missouri headwaters on July 27, 1805.[*] The skyline view they had is much the same today: Spanish Peaks to the south, Bridger Range to the east, Big Belts to the north, Tobacco Roots to the southwest and Elkhorns straight west. The Eustis and Horseshoe Hills touch down along the river courses within a mile or two

---

[*] Devoto, *Journals*, 167.

of the headwaters. Here the tributaries that are the Gallatin, Madison and Jefferson Rivers come together, forming the Missouri. When Lewis and Clark arrived, none of these terrain features had names. Wildlife still teems in this healthy riparian corridor: whitetail and mule deer, moose, the occasional black bear, elk in the surrounding hills, Merriam's wild turkey, upland birds, tons of beaver and muskrat and, of course, waterfowl.

In 1804, these species, except for whitetail, turkey and pheasant, were present, along with bison and grizzly bear. This was considered communal hunting land by Native tribes. However, the Blackfeet tended to be a bit possessive of it. Its abundance of beaver and bison wasn't lost on them. The Madison Buffalo Jump is only about ten miles southeast of here. For all intents and purposes, it was Blackfeet territory. Beaver still wreak havoc in the willows and cottonwoods. In summer, the mosquitoes can be unbearable. You will find apt and unique descriptions of this in the journals Lewis and Clark kept on the expedition. They spelled *mosquito* about ten different ways. "Muskeetor" is my personal favorite.[*]

On the heels of Lewis and Clark's discovery, fur traders descended on headwaters country en masse. Beaver in untold numbers awaited them. So did Blackfeet war parties. The dark side of this landscape is the untimely and often brutal deaths fur trappers met. Many of them remain nameless, with no chance for a proper burial. Some survived, and their names are forever etched in the history of the West: John Colter, Jim Bridger and George Drouillard, to name a few. It is this history along with wildlife that make this now-civilized region come alive today.

Jim Bridger wrote of chilling mornings—both literally and emotionally—camping at the headwaters. After a cold night of fitful sleep, he recalls coming to in the early morning hours to hear the call of "Blackfeet!" echoing through camp.[†] Attack was imminent. Fortunately, he lived to tell the tale. John Colter and his trapping partner were making their way up the Jefferson when they were ambushed by Blackfeet. His partner was killed and hacked to pieces. Colter was stripped naked and told to run. The Blackfeet wanted to get some "sport" out of him. Having met the Blackfeet before, he hid well, causing them to lose interest, then hightailed it barefoot 250 miles east to the confluence of the Yellowstone and Bighorn Rivers.

George Drouillard, famed interpreter and hunter on the Lewis and Clark Expedition and of French-Shawnee descent, met his fate here. Hiring on

---

[*] Devoto, *Journals*, 26.
[†] Haines, *Osbourne Russell's*, 71.

Beaver still roam Montana's riparian zones in healthy numbers today.

with the Missouri Fur Company after his Corps of Discovery tenure, he returned to the headwaters region in 1810. He was ambushed by Blackfeet, and his body was discovered scalped, beheaded and dismembered among the willow thickets. Surrounding his body were several dead Blackfeet, indicating he'd not gone down without a fight. Fellow trappers buried him in a hasty, unmarked grave.* Today, along the Jefferson River, a state fishing access site named in his honor sits near the site of his death.

This landscape is my backyard. For two decades, I have spent much time paddling a canoe, pitching decoys and hunting ducks on these rivers. In time, hunting this area has come to feel like a well-worn glove. I feel comfortable and at home. No familiarity breeding contempt here. That's because there is much to explore, and I find myself torn between returning to an old favorite or trying something new. Even the old spots I come to appreciate more and more with each passing year. The nature of rivers is constant change: some big, some small. Drought dries up old channels. Floods carve new ones. A good duck hole can be here this season, gone the next.

---

* Fifer and Mussulman, "George Drouillard."

One September, I began scouting for ducks two weeks out from the season. I had the itch bad, and it was to be my first season with my new black Lab, Roxy. These easy fall days are hard to beat: no mosquitoes, the leaves turning just a hint of gold. Mild breezes blow but not the hard chinooks yet to come. This time of year, the Jefferson runs low due to the rigors of irrigation by farmers and ranchers. This made wading much of it easy and allowed me to walk into some spots that in a short time, I'd have to float to.

We stepped off from the fishing access. I had the flyrod along. When we passed good holding water, I'd make a few casts. Fishing the Jeff is a "less is more" proposition. Between whirling disease in the '90s, dewatering in the summers and the slow-flowing, warmer nature of the river, fish numbers are not high, and rainbow trout are very rare. Some years, in its lower reaches, the river almost ceases to flow, with fish taking what refuge they can in the few deep holes that hold water. It's primarily a brown trout fishery, and that's what I expected to catch today. Stripping a small streamer, a swallow, below a tall cutbank, I tied into a good fish. After it took me on a couple of runs, I put a seventeen-inch rainbow to hand, my first ever on the Jeff. It was a good sign to see a fish like this that far downriver.

Releasing the fish, I heard wings overhead and spotted a pod of mallards descending below a line of willows. I walked the shallow main channel and saw where a narrow braid peeled off. Roxy perked up: she'd seen the ducks gliding down, too. This side channel turned into a chain of long, narrow sloughs due to the low water. On the first sandbar, we saw a pile of duck tracks and preened feathers—always a good sign. Several birds spooked just up ahead. Roxy whimpered, looking at me with concern about what we should do. We crept around the bend. From the next long, skinny slough, there must have been fifty mallards taking flight. Behind that bunch, another pile took to the sky from the next slough. We hunkered down in the willows to watch the birds circle. Soon they all came back. When you see a sight like this, two weeks out from duck season, the wait becomes unbearable.

Duck season arrived. I cinched the tie-down over my decoy sack on the gear rack of my one-man pontoon raft. Roxy's eyes glowed in the beam of my headlamp as she came running. She'd been sprinting to and fro in the dark, getting out the predawn Lab jitters. I settled into my rowing frame, manning the oars. Roxy perched on the right pontoon, and we shoved off into the Jeff's gentle current, headed downstream. With hay field pivot irrigators shut off and ten days of autumn rains, the river had come up a bit. A light north wind hit our faces. Roxy lifted her snout a bit to take it all in. An otter swam feet in front of us through my headlamp beam. Roxy got antsy but stayed put. The water had come up so much that the chain of sloughs teeming with ducks two weeks ago was blown out. The ducks would be elsewhere.

I steered us into a small backwater below a steep cliff just upstream of a hairpin turn in the river. It would have to do. The weather was drizzling and overcast. I pitched out decoys and tucked us under a Russian olive growing out of the bank. Soon, ducks were on the move. The first duck to land in the decoys was greeted by Roxy running out to meet it. This was one of her weaknesses: breaking before the release command. She possessed stubborn habits that took some work. In the end, it took me leashing her for the first four to five hunts of each season to get it out of her. Her eagerness and excitement were hard to contain. A bit exasperated, I missed the next mallard that cupped in. Roxy, to feel included, fetched up my spent shell, her endearing way to tell me I shot poorly. The clouds hung low and gray as the drizzle swirled in the north wind. I could see ducks on the wing in scattered flight near and far. Just upriver was where Colter and his buddy got ambushed. I've often wondered about how isolated a man must have felt on a morning like this back in 1810. A warm house and a hot breakfast, for me, is a short paddle upriver and a four-minute drive. For them, nothing like home existed for thousands of miles. You had to be ready for anything. My dog and I might spook a moose in the willows. For guys like Bridger and Drouillard, a grizzly might be feeding on a moose in those willows. Maybe a Blackfeet war party overwatched them.

The week following this hunt, a Canadian arctic cold front slammed Montana, plunging temps to twenty-five degrees below zero for a couple of days and putting the first layer of snow on the ground. I had been looking forward to some fall color as we neared the second week of duck season. All went from green and a little yellow to brown and dead on the limbs overnight. The river flowed ice, and the backwaters froze.

We have no idea how easy life is for us as hunters in the twenty-first century. From head to toe, I'm clad in a Gore-Tex jacket, neoprene waders, gloves and a few layers underneath that. In my rucksack is a thermos of hot coffee. I have a semiautomatic shotgun that will fire when wet. In 1810, a guy ate from a burlap sack of jerky and wore uninsulated buckskin, maybe a beaver hat and buffalo hide blanket or coat if worth his salt. The phrase "keep your powder dry" was basic advice for survival. Even with the best gear beaver pelts could buy, he experienced cold, hunger, filth and fear as daily, inescapable facts of life. Add to that the level of hypervigilance required to avoid Blackfeet attack and hold on to your hair, literally, and this was no place for the weak of mind or body.

One December morning, Roxy and I got a late start. We planned to float the Madison from Cobblestone to Milwaukee Bridge. Driving up Madison Road, I came upon two camo-clad hunters sitting on a canoe with no vehicle in sight. Only one of them had a shotgun. They looked wet and haggard, and it had only been daylight for an hour. I had a pretty good idea of their situation and asked where they needed a ride to. They said Cobblestone. They'd launched the canoe before daylight. Not far downriver, they flipped, losing one shotgun and a few decoys. Just hearing the story made me shiver. Fortunately, it was only in the thirties that morning. Much colder, and things could have been serious for them. In 1810, there was no fellow trapper coming along in a pickup to help you if your canoe flipped.

While my pontoon raft is a bit more stable than a canoe, I can't resist the utility and romance of a canoe for duck hunting. Paddling one on a river takes you back in time—and I can squeeze in a bigger decoy sack. But it pays to be smart with it and wear a life jacket. One doesn't duck hunt in a canoe on moving water lightly. I confine use of it to early season hunts. Mine isn't fancy. I bought it from a friend for twenty dollars and put a sweet camo spray paint job on it. It has a couple of small leaks that marine silicone handles just fine. The first season with it, I discovered a special spot not far from the confluence of the headwaters.

Beaver had been hard at work helping me out that summer. They dammed a creek that flowed from a sharp bend in the Madison through a cottonwood island and dumped out just above the Jeff. Downstream of the beaver dam, the creek was the perfect depth for mallards and other puddlers. Along one side was a steep cutbank that had enough ground at the bottom for a hunter to craft a makeshift blind from willows and driftwood. Getting there was a little western. The confluence currents swirled and pushed hard. Multiple drownings have occurred just downstream. There are deep holes just below the creek mouth. The sketchiest part is crossing the swift current of the Madison. It only takes about twenty seconds or less, but the feel of that stiff flow against the entirety of the canoe's length tells you there's no room for error. Once you're tight to the bank on the other side, the easy current puts you right in the mouth of the creek, which has no discernible flow. One hunter and a dog, no problem. Two hunters and a dog with gear is another matter. All done in the dark with headlamps.

My good friend and duck-hunting pal Alex Betz has a primal fear of canoes. He's not afraid of much else. This guy battled insurgents in Iraq, handcuffed outlaw bikers as a state trooper and climbed Granite Peak, the highest mountain in Montana. He's a tough guy. It was dark thirty at the put-in. I'd got the canoe loaded. Roxy was antsy, running around, suggesting it was time to get paddling. Alex was still by the truck pacing around, fiddling with gear, buckling and unbuckling his wader belt. When I asked what he was doing, all I could get out of him was, "I don't like canoes, man." He said this in a very calm but genuine way. It was news to me that morning. I told him I'd keep Roxy at the truck, run him across first, then come back for the dog: that should make things less tippy.

We got in and paddled across with no problems. Depositing him on the bank just past the mouth of the creek, I could see his legs shaking and his relief to be on solid ground. Not a word was said the whole time we paddled. He offered to get the dekes out while I went back for Roxy. We ended up having a good hunt that morning. We pulled in a few mallards with my new jerk string rig. Fall colors had come in on the cottonwoods and willows. It came time to load up and head back across the river. In daylight, things didn't feel so ominous. Alex let me know back at the truck that he would continue to duck hunt with me but that he was never getting in that canoe again. He then confided a bad experience in a canoe on moving water one summer. No need for details. It was a bad experience. Fair enough.

Canoeing into a blind near the Missouri headwaters. *Brian Stoner.*

Sun setting on Freezout Lake.

Z canals habitat project at Freezout Lake.

Alex and Cassie hunting at Freezout Lake Wildlife Management Area.

Cassie retrieving a wigeon, Freezout Lake Wildlife Management Area.

Alex Betz, Duke, Roxy and author with a sub-zero limit of mallards.

Roxy at attention in the blind.

Sub-zero limit, Pacific Flyway, Montana.

Boat blind hunt, Madison River.

Canoes allow access to hard-to-reach sloughs along river corridors.

Late season on the Gallatin.

Hunters enjoying a pleasant fall day, Red Rock Lakes National Wildlife Refuge.

Pitching decoys, Red Rock Lakes National Wildlife Refuge.

Sunrise in the blind, Centennial Valley.

Retrieves in low-water years can be a slog for dogs. *Jamie Young*

Speculum plumage on drake pintail, one of the ways to identify species at close range.

Hunting with vintage side-by-sides brings the spirit of the Old West into the blind.

Alex and Roxy fine-tuning the decoys at sunrise.

Jim Hansen and Fancy. *Roger Parker.*

A mild, sunny January day, Montana's Bighorn River.

One of many waterfowl production areas on the Hi-Line.

Decoys at dawn on the Hi-Line.

Mixed bag early season limit.

An early season bag on the Hi-Line.

Stalking wood ducks, Milk River oxbow.

Dan Cook and Brownie on a successful morning at Ennis Lake.

Ducks grilled fast and rare eat best.

Hunters pitching decoys, southwest Montana. *Jamie Young.*

Centennial Range looming over decoys. *Jamie Young*

Heavy action in the duck blind, southwest Montana. *Jamie Young*

This spot could be good on the right day. Rainy, cool mornings seemed best. One morning, Roxy and I paddled into the mouth of the creek. On cue, a beaver slapped the water with his tail to say hello. As I swung my headlamp beam back to the prow of the canoe, I saw two sets of eyes staring back at me. Each set was about twelve inches wide. One was about six feet off the ground, the other about three feet. Moose! A cow and calf moose! Not a good situation when your canoe is heading straight for the bank they are bedded on. I did what I could to back up and give us some space. Crowding a cow moose with a calf can be just as dangerous as surprising a grizzly. The few seconds seemed to last forever. The cow stood up and took off in the opposite direction, calf in tow. Roxy shook with excitement but never broke, following my calm command, "Stay." Breathing a sigh of relief, I beached the canoe and got to work pitching decoys.

Roxy and I hunkered against the bank. Things shaped up well at shooting time with a flight of eight to ten mallards responding to a light tug on my jerk string. I culled one out of that flight but should have taken two. Soon another flight of as many birds swung wide and reacted to the jerk string. Roxy sat stone-still with only slight movements of her head tracking the flight's every move, just waiting for one to drop. At the shot, she launched and went for a mallard hen that fell straight across from us, fetching it back in short order. I gave her a gentle slap on the torso and massaged her head. Good dog!

More ducks came in, and I cut one that fell atop the cutbank just behind us. Roxy was up and on it before I could do anything. We did our best to stay within the legal bounds of the stream access law. Standing up to keep an eye on Roxy, I saw her at the edge of the cutbank, duck in her mouth, right next to a moose shed antler, a pretty good one for this area. As the morning shoot wound down, the birds dispersed; the clouds and rain lifted. It was back to a sunny Indian summer morning. Loaded in the canoe, we paddled out to the Madison, then upriver to our crossing and take-out.

It always amazed me how interesting things could get there, in a matter of minutes, from the second I shoved off in a canoe. Thinking of Lewis, Clark, Drouillard, Bridger and Colter, I wondered what their thoughts must have been each time they shoved off for the day. I'm sure each of them had many an occasion to wonder if this was the last time they'd slip a canoe into a river ever again. I must admit that every time I hunt this spot, I have the sense that a lot could go wrong if I'm not careful. Most of it is in my head. This was indeed real and true for early explorers and mountain men.

Beaver dam near the Missouri headwaters.

Not long after duck season a few years ago, I crossed the Madison on I-90 headed to work. Winter had settled in, and much of it was covered in ice. Near the lip of an ice sheet where an open channel coursed, I spotted a large beaver with a long willow branch in its teeth. I laughed to myself. I thought of Lewis and Clark, all the mountain men who followed in their footsteps, the many who died and the eventual significant changes the fur trade brought to this region. We now live very civilized lives where much barbarity once existed. I go out in my canoe, hunt ducks and return home safe and dry most days. And it all started because of that brown furbearer sitting on the ice, gnawing a willow branch.

CHAPTER 7

WEST OF THE DIVIDE

An earlier version of "West of the Divide" was published in the Winter 2014 issue of Montana Sporting Journal.

The bull moose browsed on willow as the late autumn sun illuminated the golden leaves shimmering in the light, cold breeze. Arctic grayling darted back and forth in the gin-clear stream among the gargantuan ungulate's legs. Overhead, tundra swans and flights of geese headed south toward the vertical north slope of a snow-capped mountain range. Slightly west lay a pair of sprawling, shallow lakes hosting all the major Pacific Flyway species: pintail, mallard, gadwall, wigeon, teal, canvasback, you name it. In this land, winter's breath is never far away. One might assume this place is north of the sixty-sixth parallel. The herd of pronghorn grazing the shortgrass prairie nearby that day dispelled that notion, contrasting with the area's tundra-esque landscape. Closer to the mountains, a bull elk coveted his harem among golden quaking aspen. So goes an average fall day in the Centennial Valley, home to Red Rock Lakes National Wildlife Refuge.

Fall is short for this wetland pearl sitting at 6,600 feet. Waterfowl season opens barely in time for hunters to get a crack at the birds before ice up. Freezeout typically occurs by the third weekend in October. Water was low that year—so low, in fact, that our canoes remained in camp. Our best hope was to find a small pocket of water off the main lake to set decoys in. There was two inches of water in most places and two feet of mud below that. Roxy would be earning her keep that opening weekend. After much scouting the day before the opener, it appeared birds would be just about anywhere. We were told by the refuge warden that this was a slow year. Most seasons, a lot more birds are here, he said.

Opening morning, we stepped into the cool darkness, decoy bags shouldered, shotguns slung. Walking for probably a mile, we arrived at our chosen hole to see less water than yesterday—unexpected. Overnight, the wind had blown water twenty to thirty yards from shore. The hole had the appearance of an exposed tidal flat. With little time to adjust our plans before shooting time, we slogged through the knee- to thigh-deep mud to the water's edge, hastily deploying decoys. We weren't sure how this would play out, so the spread remained conservative. As is typical with Labs in early season, Roxy was having trouble focusing. As she slogged out into the mud behind me, her effort suggested she was offering some assistance with placing dekes. She barreled out ahead of us and back several times. She saw the guns, smelled the water, heard decoys clunking in the sack. She knew what was about to happen.

Dawn crept in, and before us lay perhaps the most impressive backdrop for a duck hunt any of us had ever seen. The water on the lake was dead calm as the Centennial Range towered overhead, capped with a shroud of low-hanging clouds. Alex was set up in a patch of cattails off to the right while Adam, Roxy and I sat tight in a makeshift blind, waiting for shooting time to arrive. Alex was whispering rather loudly at us. We couldn't understand what he was saying. We looked left and saw three teal sitting on the water not far from our dekes. I pointed to clue Alex and Adam in. Exasperated, Alex shouted, "That's what I was tryin' to tell ya!" At that, the teal got airborne, and I goosed the first shot of the season.

"Nice shootin'!" Alex jabbed at the top of his lungs.

Not long after, a pod of gadwall swooped in, surprising us. Two fell at our shots. Who hit 'em? Who knows. Flights began to come in sporadically. We took our shots as they came. Roxy slogged through the chest-deep mud unfettered. On one retrieve, one hundred yards plus on a gadwall hen, she lunge-sprinted to the bird and, on turning around, made a slightly slower return. If it was me, I'd probably have done the same thing. Her work for the day was not yet done.

Red Rock Lakes is one of the most remote wildlife refuges in the lower forty-eight that's reachable by vehicle. As with any good remote hunting location, there is no short, easy way to get here. The nearest large town, Dillon, is roughly one hundred miles away. Often described as the most beautiful wildlife refuge in the nation, it boasts the largest high-altitude wetland in the Greater Yellowstone Ecosystem. Like most national wildlife refuges, Red Rock Lakes was set aside in the beginning for a specific purpose: helping to restore populations of trumpeter swan.[*]

Once populations rebounded on the refuge, it was used as a conduit for restocking efforts throughout the Midwest and the mountain states. As a result, a truly remarkable piece of habitat was preserved that remains a living testament to the key benchmark of a healthy habitat: biodiversity. Of course, we were there to hunt ducks, but the array of wildlife that calls Red Rock Lakes home is staggering. Over 250 species of birds can be found here. Every large mammal species in the northern Rockies hangs its hat in the area. A grizzly bear wandering through your decoys is not out of the question. The week prior to our arrival, a refuge advisory went out that a grizzly migration was underway through the area. A large number of cattle had died on a ranch west of the refuge. Once word got out, area bruins converged to take advantage. We never saw one, and that was OK.

When the refuge was established in 1935, much of it still bore the marks of the homesteading that was underway at the turn of the century. Management of the refuge has always focused on returning it to the wild, natural character it once had. This job has been done well. Other than the refuge headquarters on the southwest end, there are no maintained services in an area encompassing over sixty-five thousand acres. Campgrounds are few, and the refuge seldom sees visitors other than at peak times of the year, mostly during hunting season. One spring, Mom and I drove down to hunt birds with cameras and binoculars. We could count on one hand the number of people we saw. Even though the campground was near capacity that opening weekend of duck season with Alex and Adam, there was still more than enough elbow room. Once in the blind, a hunter feels about as far away from civilization as they can get, even if they're within a mile of a road.

By eleven o'clock that morning, the bird action had slowed down a little and the temperature had climbed past fifty. We had twelve birds to hand and thought we'd return to camp for a midday break, get the birds plucked and marinating for dinner, then head back out for an afternoon hunt. The other half of our hunting party, Wade, Jamie and Cade, had worse luck than we did. They set up in the middle of open water, and most of the birds they saw were high-fliers—marginal pass shooting at best. After discussing our range of options, we decided to all head back to where Alex, Adam and I hunted that morning. Jamie and Wade opted to leave their guns in camp and bring their cameras instead. Cade, Wade's son, not old enough to hunt yet, helped us haul gear.

---

* U.S. Fish and Wildlife Service, "Red Rock Lakes."

Decoys on a rare non-windy day, Centennial Valley.

On arrival, we decided to increase the size of our decoy spread. Adam and I drew the short straws and slogged out into the knee-deep muck. Each of us had a full sack of decoys. To make matters easier, we each pulled decoys from the other's sack to avoid hauling in extra weight in the form of mud on our decoy bags. We also set out a wind-driven spinner decoy. Motorized decoys of any kind are prohibited on federal wildlife refuges. As our hunt progressed, we came to learn nature's subtle and overt indifference toward humans here. For starters, low water made it practically impossible to use our canoes. Low water also brought us in closer contact with the alkaline-laden mud, which, once dried on your equipment and skin, pretty much stays there even after a good washing. By day two, our hands were so dried out they began to crack.

Wind is an overt factor that, when combined with this unique terrain, causes problems. As in many parts of Montana, wind is a fact of life here. Given the altitude and the fact that this broad, open swath of wetland lies along the only mountain range running east to west in the state, the prevailing southwest winds tend to funnel along the north slope at breakneck speeds when weather patterns shift. As the afternoon progressed, the wind picked up—a lot. High winds of this nature do a couple of things that are uniquely problematic for the duck hunter: (1) They create dispersal problems for one's shot pattern, especially at longer ranges—and oftentimes the ducks are being blown away from you by the wind as you're shooting. (2) As seen earlier, in low-water conditions, they can blow water right out of your spot, leaving you with a mudflat to hunt over. There is also the ethical question: Where is your bird going to go once it hits the water? Will your dog be able to get to the bird in time? If you don't have a dog, there's no way you'll get to the bird before it blows halfway across the lake—I don't care how fast you're running through this mud. You have to take this into consideration when picking your spot. At a certain point, it's simply absurd to hunt in winds beyond thirty miles per hour.

Despite the uptick in wind speeds, things still seemed promising. As I sat next to Alex on my stool, getting situated, he noticed me putting my earplugs in.

"Oh boy!" he shouted. "Matt's here!"—referring to my earplug voice volume. As he doesn't wear earplugs himself, our conversations could be somewhat interesting to the casual observer—especially if we were on a street corner and not in a duck blind. Wade burrowed down in the grass while Jamie donned his ghillie suit, which tucked him into the surroundings better than anything we had.

Wigeon showed up, and we got a crack at them. It's always good to see the old baldpate. Wily birds, they are beautiful and, once in hand, a delight to eat. Roxy moved slow, working her way back with this wigeon. Her spirit was strong, but her legs were beginning to feel the toll of a full day pushing through mud. Covered in muck, wigeon in mouth, she heaved herself onto the bank after the last few feet of the retrieve. I told the guys that I was going to shut her down for the day. She'd more than earned her pay grabbing birds out of that quagmire.

With an hour of daylight left, we called it a hunt for the opener. In all, the crew had brought down about twenty birds. We'd have plenty to eat that night. We'd been looking forward to an evening of sitting around the campfire recounting the day's events, enjoying a good cigar. Wind preempted that plan. I cooked up the day's kill marinated in lemon juice, olive oil and rosemary. Quickly seared on the grill and rare, they went quickly around the table in Wade's camper alongside mashed spuds.

That night, we got a visit from a special guest. Alex and I were finishing up grilling the last of the birds when a flashlight beam hit us.

"Federal agent, need to check your ducks."

It was David Farmer, the local refuge warden: a super nice guy but very businesslike in his approach.

"Have at it," I said. "We've cooked and ate up most of 'em. You know who you'd better check is my buddy, Adam Pankratz. He's in that camper right there."

David laughed. Adam, a fellow game warden, worked with David on occasion. David had no idea he was down hunting this weekend, though. Wardens can be secretive about their hunting activities to perpetuate the myth that we never get to do it. Sometimes this is true. Work can get in the way of it. But like anything else, if it's important enough, we make time for it. David poked his head in to say hi. Adam was bearing down on a wigeon leg. David bid us goodnight and went to check other camps.

Alex turned to me after he drove away. "Boy, he's kinda sneaky! Coming up in the dark like that. I felt like we'd been caught drinking underage or something."

"It makes sense," I said. "If you wanna get the drop on folks keeping too many birds, best to check 'em in camp at night after they've maybe had a beer or two and have their guard down. Risky, I suppose, depending on who you're dealing with. He probably got a good nap in this afternoon. We've been slaving in the marsh all day!"

"Sneaky!" Alex repeated.

Next day we awoke to howling wind, stiffer than yesterday. Undeterred, we headed out to where we'd left our decoy spread the evening before. In the back of my mind, I hoped all the knots on the anchor lines had held. Amazingly, the wind-powered spinner was still standing when we arrived, and all dekes were there. (I should note that regulations have since changed on the refuge, requiring hunters to remove decoys daily now.) Hunkered in our blinds, we awaited legal shooting time. Birds don't fly much on day two around here. For the most part, they're rafted up on the upper lake, where no hunting is allowed. We managed a few shots at some teal. The last one that went down, Roxy made a valiant effort to retrieve. In the end, I called her off, as the bird was swiftly blown across the lake and I had no idea how bad the mud got on the other side. She wasn't going to quit going for it. We lost that one and decided it was too windy to continue. Gathering up dekes, we hauled the gear back to camp and made ready to head home.

October the following year, we returned, this time with a pile of kids: Alex had his two girls, McKenzie and Lauren; Wade and Jamie's boys, Cade and Liam, were there; and with me was my late friend's son, Ethan. Ethan's dad, Amos Ridenour, had been killed in a tragic climbing accident the year previous. We had been coworkers, hunted and fished together. Not knowing what else to do, I took Ethan hunting and fishing with me as much as possible. He fit right into the outdoor life and, game for anything, was a great buddy to have along. There were three dogs: Roxy, Duke (Alex's 120-pound tank of a yellow Lab) and Argus, a drahthaar that belonged to Wade's brother, Sean. Wade was on extended babysitting duty while his brother was overseas on a contracting job. First order of business the Friday before opener was to stake a claim and get decoys out. The great thing about having kids along is they can be helpful in the decoy chore department. If you're putting decoys out the afternoon before, time isn't as precious a resource as it is the morning of.

Alex wouldn't get there until that night. The rest of us hauled out decoy sacks to the same spot we hunted last year. The surrounding marsh was bathed in autumn sunlight; the temp was about fifty-five degrees and calm. It was nice day to do just about anything, but setting out the first spread of the season was the best way to spend it. The lower lake had a lot more water than last year. In our spot, there was easily six inches. This would make hunting conditions a little more promising as the decoys would be sitting in water, not mud with a little water here and there.

The grass was higher, too, which made for good concealment. The refuge is on a rest/rotation grazing system, which leases ground to area ranchers. Last year was a grazing year, so concealment was sparse. This year, especially with the good moisture conditions we had, the grass was waist high. Wade hauled in his Fast Grass boat blind, without the boat. We were able erect it into local grass well, and it made for a wicked-looking duck blind—in that you didn't notice it. Hopefully, the birds wouldn't either.

In all, we put out about two dozen dekes with a wind spinner. The route in had us crossing a narrow but deep ditch, which required piggybacking kids. I was able to fit Ethan in the sled with one decoy sack and ferry him across while I waded. Getting the decoys out, it felt good to be ahead of the game. With that out of the way, we could kick back in camp and watch the sunset over Centennial Valley and the lakes. The stars twinkled to life at the last rays of twilight. About that time, I saw headlights bouncing toward the campground on the dirt road. Here comes Alex. Hauling his fifth wheel, they came down the long way: I-15 to Lima, then east.

Up at five, Ethan was ready to go. We got coffee made and breakfast served. Things were on schedule. Alex and I hunted together with the kids and let Wade and Jamie handle their own plans. They usually hunted with us, but depending on how much whiskey came with them, they may

Opening day bag on Red Rock Lakes National Wildlife Refuge.

or may not get going with a rip in the morning. Ethan and I were headed out the door when Alex informed me they would be delayed—something about one of the girls not being quite ready. I told him we'd get the blind warmed up. Ethan and I struck out. Wade and Jamie's camper was dark and quiet when we passed.

The skies were sharply clustered with stars, bright in the crisp twenty-five-degree air. A light coat of frost blanketed the grass. Roxy had an air of friskiness about her as she sprinted to and fro in front of us, then behind us like a cutting horse. We were in the blind and getting settled in ten minutes ahead of shooting time. We had a grand view as dawn awakened across the Centennial ridgeline and poured over the valley and through the cattails along the lakeshore. There was not a lick of wind except for the occasional light, intermittent breeze from the sun hitting the air. The sun burned orange as it climbed over the valley, and we could see swarms of ducks airborne above the upper lake.

"Take it all in, Ethan. This is what we're here for. That right there."

He nodded with a look halfway between a grin and awe.

That scene alone gave us the sensation it would be a banner morning. The sight of ducks like that on opening morning? Epic. I tried to imagine it through Ethan's eyes. There was the distinct possibility it was unlike anything he'd ever seen—and he'd never forget it, either. First impressions work that way.

The calm had passed, and now we were starting to get birds flying around us—mostly passing shots, a lot like last year. About seven thirty, I spotted Alex and his girls headed toward us. Then Wade popped up in the grass out of nowhere a hundred yards away. He'd gone ahead of us but got off his bearings and ended up fighting through some waist-deep holes near the lakeshore and started the morning off where he was. Soon enough, we were shoulder to shoulder in the blind: three hunters, three kids and three dogs.

The morning flyout slowed to a crawl. It seemed that most of the birds were rafted up on the upper lake, where, of course, there is no hunting. By ten o'clock, we had four birds to bag, three teal and a ruddy. One was a blue-wing, a rarity at that time of year. We lost a couple of cripples in the grass. Roxy, now ten years old, did her best slogging through the muck. She couldn't make up for what we lacked in shooting. By noon, we were back in camp, where we'd mull over the afternoon plan. It was much warmer and milder this year, and the birds just weren't that active. Our thoughts turned

Roxy bringing in a hen gadwall.

Author picks up the last deke, Red Rock Lakes National Wildlife Refuge. *Jamie Young.*

toward tomorrow morning and where we might go. With water in the lake, I wanted to make use of the canoe and explore.

About three o'clock, Ethan and I loaded up some decoys and struck out east to see where we might hunt in the morning. The water was glass calm as we glided over the muddy flats of the lower lake. Ethan's head moved left, then right as he surveyed all the sights there were to see. Coots skittered back and forth in the cattails. I settled us on a point beyond which was a secluded arm of the lake. No birds spooked out of it, but there were none around to speak of anywhere on the lower lake. I showed Ethan how to pitch out dekes and space them. He was a quick study and all smiles. It was good to see him smiling. Only a year out from his father's untimely death and so young, he was working through a lot and still processing. For age seven, he was so resilient. We pitched probably a dozen and a half blocks. In the gentle warmth of Indian summer, this was enjoyable labor. The processes of duck hunting can be as fun as the shooting, in the right circumstances.

Early the following morning, we slid the canoe into the water under brilliant stars in a moonless sky. I only needed my headlamp to make sure we had all our gear loaded. In the distance we could see the black silhouettes of the Centennial, Henry and Madison Ranges. It was so quiet. The only sound was that of the paddle pushing water. Roxy sat alert but calm between me and Ethan. On banking the canoe, Roxy was out and doing her usual morning sprints through the grass. We slipped into our blind and were treated to another epic dawn. The water was mirror perfect as the sun broke over the mountains and lit up the brown grass and cattails. Ducks were strikingly absent. We heard nary a shot for the next two hours. Nothing even flew high. At midmorning we called it and gathered up dekes.

Weather this nice, no gunfire to move 'em and all the food they needed on the upper lake meant it was a slow day for everybody, no matter where you were on the refuge. Speaking for myself, I could come out here every opening weekend expecting to get skunked and still look forward to it. The backdrop must be seen to be believed. There is no place finer to go through the motions of duck hunting.

CHAPTER 8

DUCK SKIFF DAN

A light south wind blew in our faces as the boat motored into the morning darkness. The sweet smell of fall-cured leaves and grass sifted through my nostrils. Dan maneuvered his duck skiff across the south flats of Ennis Lake with precision. He'd done this enough that he knew exactly when to adjust course to avoid bottoming out in mud or fouling the motor in weeds. Brownie, his American water spaniel, stood on the bow, ears floating in the breeze. Only occasionally did Dan ask me to pop the Q-Beam on and sweep the shoreline. This was to make sure he didn't pass up his preferred duck blind.

It's one thing to float hunt a small river or traipse into a marsh accessible by foot. These affairs are simple and straightforward. But hunting big water in the mountains via boat is where the waterfowler's experience matters. Understanding how and when the birds use the water is essential. Then there is understanding the lake's relationship with weather and that of both to the surrounding mountain ranges. Not understanding this part will get you into real trouble. In this regard, Dan was a pro.

Soon Dan let off the throttle and we drifted up to the blind. We offloaded dry bags and shotguns under the willows. Next, we got to work pitching puddler decoys on either side of the blind. The beauty in hunting Ennis Lake is that you get a good variety of puddlers and divers. So it pays to put out a good-size spread that's a mix of both species. Once the puddler dekes were out, it was time for the diver string. We climbed back in the boat and motored a short distance from the blind. Dan put his diver gang line on about eighty feet of cotton braided line with grappling hook weights at both ends. He had oversized line clips tied to each decoy. As he rolled out the diver line, he'd clip on a decoy with assembly line efficiency. In less than ten minutes, the diver line was out and bobbing in the light chop.

The view from our duck blind was quintessential Montana. Ennis Lake sits at just over 4,800 feet of elevation in the shadow of the Madison Range to the east, flanked by the looming peaks of the Tobacco Roots in the west, surrounded by sage-studded foothills to the north and fed by the deltaic, braided upper Madison River flowing into it from the south. This lake is as scenic as it gets and has decent duck hunting in the area come fall if things line up right and you know how to hunt it.

The lake is an obvious spot to hunt waterfowl, but uncertainty about how to approach it kept me at bay—until I met Dan Cook. Dan is a duck hunter of the first order and has been hunting the lake well over two decades. The two of us come from opposite ends of the Mississippi Flyway. While I was raised on its southern wintering grounds in Louisiana, Dan cut his teeth hunting ducks along the flyway's namesake river in southern Minnesota. He came to Montana in the late 1980s when it still had some elbow room— before movies and later, a TV series, followed by pandemic chaos, ushered in hordes of van-driving refugees who rediscovered the outdoors and descended from all directions.

Hunting and fishing with Dan is special. It's not often you get in a boat that the guy you're going with built. To look at his duck skiff, you'd never think it was built in Dan's garage. "Custom factory" might describe the boat's look better. Dan built it in his garage over a long winter, the way a duck hunter who knows how to build boats would do it: just wide enough to accommodate three hunters yet narrow enough to get in the tight spots duck hunters tend to go. It has under-bench storage that will hold small ice chests, blind bags and guns, minimizing clutter above deck. His decoy system is meticulous. The diver string dekes are in a slotted decoy bag, with the remaining puddlers in two Texas-rigged bunches hooked to the bow with carabiners. We're talking dialed in.

Hunting Ennis Lake, like any large body of water in Montana, is a weather game. Of course, you want some weather to push birds down. More importantly, you want to enjoy the hunt, not just survive it. While a little foul weather isn't a bad thing, you don't want to get caught out there when the wind gets to ripping. If the winds are out of the southwest, which is the norm, getting out isn't too bad, as you can skirt the lakeshore to the nearest launch. If you come in from the north side, you have it at your back, at least.

Stiff north wind? Forget it. The ducks are all coming in from behind you, and the ride out is going to be western.

With Dan, I never worried about that. He would always make a call the night before based on current weather conditions. We'd link up about five o'clock in the morning in Norris, then head to the lake. Dan knew the course to the blind by heart and, once underway, maneuvered through weed beds and around the shallow flats known for fouling boat motors. We always went during the week. There was never a line at the boat ramp, maybe another hunter or two. Weekends can be crowded, so it's a race to get to your favored spot. However, having hunters scattered around the lake and upriver does keep the ducks moving a little longer. Dan had everything timed perfectly.

With the decoys out, we were back in the blind with fifteen to twenty minutes to go before shooting time. I sipped coffee while Dan fired up one of his favored stogies. Brownie sat dutifully at his side. I must admit, hunting a spaniel took me some getting used to, as I've been a Lab man my entire life and always will be. But Brownie is steady on the retrieve and has an easygoing disposition. Like every hunting dog, she has her dark side and would try to help herself to a fresh duck now and then.

By then, I'd hunted Ennis Lake with Dan five or six times. An exciting aspect of hunting Ennis Lake is the duck variety. The size of this body of water and its location make it a regional funneling point for migrating waterfowl in the flyway. In that regard, you never know what kind of hunt it will be. There are always gadwall and mallard to go around. But sometimes things get teal heavy. One hunt, we shot almost exclusively widgeon. In the midst of steady puddler shooting, the intermittent bluebill, redhead or canvasback can fall into the bag. I've even spotted harlequin ducks here as the ice encroaches on open water later in the season.

The crowd that hunts here consists of the usual variety for a favored local hot spot, including the college-age crowd from Bozeman, many of whom set up at spots around the lake where they can walk in or paddle with a canoe. Our hearts go out to these guys because Dan and I were there, once upon a time. You've got barely enough money for gas, let alone anything else. You've probably got Dad or Granddad's shotgun, whatever decoys you and your buddies could pool together or what Dad would let you have, and if the stars line up right, somebody in the group has a johnboat with few to no leaks in it. Maybe it even has a running motor. Then there's no limit to the trouble young duck hunters can find themselves in.

However, these days, with shifts in the economic demographic of the student body at MSU in Bozeman, it's not unusual to see this crowd showing up with eighteen-foot aluminum skiffs powered by forty-horse jet motors towed by a brand-new three-quarter-ton Ford or Chevy on top of a lift kit, both looking like they just rolled off the showroom floor. Odds are there are California or Washington State license plates on the towing rig. Just gettin' in a little duck hunting before class. This wasn't the case twenty years ago. Still, I'm touched when I see a young waterfowler show up with a nonmotorized layout boat and a diver decoy string bulging in the back of a used half-ton pickup. Somebody was taking good care of this kid when they introduced them to duck hunting.

In my experience as a game warden, it's also with this crowd you'll find the early shooters, unplugged shotguns and the occasional overlimit. In most cases, it's a matter of not reading the regs, taking their friend's word or getting carried away on the rare good day. Not that it's always young people, but most of the time it is. And most of them learn their lesson the first time. One case I know of: a fellow game warden responded to address a nonresident lone shooter who was confused about duck season dates and went out hunting on the lake a month early. He certainly had the lake all to himself that morning. As far as the unplugged shotguns go, in my experience, it's almost always a case of a new hunter hunting with a family heirloom vintage shotgun that Dad or Grandad told them was good to go and they assumed was plugged. Many of these guns didn't originally come with plugs. The easiest field fix for this problem is an unsharpened no. 2 pencil. It's the perfect length for a plug. I've always got a handful in the work truck to help a guy out after I've taken care of the administrative side of things. I can't say I've ever checked a duck hunter with an unplugged shotgun who had an overlimit of ducks—not even a limit, most times. In almost every case, it's a matter of ignorance.

Dan and I are all about getting young duck hunters pointed in the right direction. At FWP, he often had college interns or warden trainees who were aspiring duck hunters with the want but not the boat, decoys and know-how to hunt a place like Ennis. Dan worked seasonally at the Montana Department of Fish, Wildlife and Parks, spraying noxious weeds in summer, then tending the front office in fall before he migrated south to Florida. He worked with a lot of young people figuring out their lives, a few of them avid or aspiring duck hunters. Dan helped many of them with a lot of no-nonsense life coaching as well as inviting them on an occasional duck hunt. Dan and I had more than a few of these young folks join us on a hunt, and it was always fun having that youthful enthusiasm along for the ride.

Dan Cook and Brownie motoring in from a morning hunt, western Montana.

As for the rest of the Ennis Lake crowd, there is the fly-fishing crowd from Bozeman or Ennis, many of them fishing guides in summer, who will drop a small motor on their drift boat or raft or even row out onto the lake. You'll see only a handful of these folks from year to year, and they never take over in force. That leaves the hardcore waterfowling crowd. Dan and I consider ourselves part of this problem. These hunters are serious, and you have to have a sense of when they hunt if you want to get to your blind unoccupied, because they know where the good blinds are. Hardcore duck hunters can be constricted by the five-day workweek, but more often, they will hunt as the weather and migration rhythms dictate, flexing their work schedule around things if possible. You never know when these guys will be your competition. This crew knows the lake, knows when and how to hunt it and will be launching jet-powered boats with pop-up boat blinds ready to go right next to you at dark thirty. This can be part of the energy that makes waterfowl hunting fun, when everyone is respectful and courteous. It keeps the ducks moving on days when they otherwise don't have to.

With our decoy spread out, Dan and I settled into the blind. He preferred opening days like this one, sometime after opening weekend of the season. Some years, depending on bird numbers, local and nonlocal hunting pressure elsewhere on the opener will trigger mini migrations of ducks. In the Pacific

Flyway, we are blessed with an abundance of birds and a generous bag limit of seven ducks. There are, of course, limits on certain species, like redhead, scaup and canvasback, which fluctuate year to year, but for the most part you can fill a limit with mallard, gadwall, widgeon and teal. Out to our front, we could hear birds splashing water, probably coots rafted up in the middle of the lake. I set up a jerk string just out in front of the blind. Dan turned on a couple of spinning-wing dekes as well. The skies were partly overcast, the air a cool but comfortable forty-six degrees. Soon, wingbeats overhead signaled the morning flyout was on. Legal shooting time came, and we locked shut our over/under shotguns and sat ready.

I could hear the soft whistle of widgeon out there. I tugged lightly on the jerk rig while playing the call, trying to match notes with their whistles. Dan and I saw the flight was much closer than we realized as they hit the brakes and cupped out in front of us. We opened up: I folded two, and Dan had a clean miss, unusual for him. Brownie collected the two widgeon, and we hunkered back down. More birds were on the move out front. More ducks piled into our spread. Dan connected and got on the board, making a clean run with his double. We now had widgeon, gadwall and one blue-winged teal. The duck strap was beginning to look a little crowded. At 8:15, I had shot my final bird for a one-man limit. I cracked my gun and left it to Dan, who had just a few more to go. I tended the jerk string and kept up my calling regimen.

It isn't always the guy who limits out first that wins. My bag was nearly all widgeon and gadwall: a feast fit for a king, trimmed in white fat. Dan, however, was shaking things up as he approached limiting out. He got the one and only greenhead of the day for his sixth bird. Then a lone diver duck buzzed the decoys, and Dan closed out his limit with a beautiful redhead drake. Dan exuded happiness like a duck in water, all smiles—not only because of the redhead, though. This was probably the most retrieving action Brownie had gotten in a while. It was the first time Dan and I limited out here that I could remember. It was seldom we got skunked, but hunts tended to be tough and ended by the clock, not the limit.

The kicker about this morning, however, was that as we hunted, Dan informed me that he and his wife had just sold their house. After thirty years of life in Montana, they would be headed home to Minnesota. Weary of the place Bozeman had become, they had aging parents to care for, and the current housing market was too ridiculous to pass up (the house didn't make it a day on the market, with bidding wars to boot). I felt thankful both of us could have such a good hunt. You always hope there will be more hunts with good friends, but you'd best appreciate the good times as they happen. Once you're separated by distance like this, especially the older you get, the hunts get fewer and farther between. I would bask in this moment for a while. Ennis Lake will miss you, Dan Cook.

CHAPTER 9

CROW COUNTRY

Wingbeats whistled along the river's course as a flight of goldeneye searched for slack water to land in. It was midafternoon, and the January-bare limbs of towering cottonwoods loomed over the banks of the Bighorn River just south of Hardin. It was the second-to-last day of duck season in Montana's Zone 2 of the Central Flyway. The birds had been hunted hard and showed it. We got occasional flyovers by small flights of mallard that slowed down to check us out, made a pass, maybe two, then moved on. They'd seen it all before. Me and my friend Dale Spartas were set up in a perfect little back eddy off the main river. With the mild weather over the last week, the water was completely open. Our decoy spread was a shade shy of two dozen, with some goose floaters and bigfoots on the gravel bar for good measure. Callie, Dale's black Lab, was ever eager to go to work at nine years of age with two days of season left.

Our plan was to sit until sunset and see what transpired. Dale's friend Scott owned the river frontage we were hunting on, with about 240 acres of cut corn behind us. When we showed up, he and his hunting party were preparing to depart. He advised us that the birds were wary and the majority of flight activity wasn't until after legal shooting time ended. Still, we were hopeful we'd get some action. Hunkered into the willows and grass along the back eddy, we took turns calling and sat ready.

Hunting the Bighorn presents challenges on a couple fronts. The prime stretch of river is mostly on the Crow Indian Reservation, and non-tribal members must stay below the high-water mark, as only the river is public access in this area unless you have access to non-tribal deeded land. Our hunting setup was a unique situation. Most hunters must access the river through one of several fishing access sites: Afterbay, Three Mile, Bighorn, Mallards and Two Leggins. A fair number of waterfowl hunters float the river in a drift boat or raft. The hardcore folks run jet or surface drive boats up and down the river to key hunting locations and set up decoys. Dale and I saw several of these outfits cruising up and down the river that day. Several fishing lodges and outfitters based on the Bighorn offer guided waterfowl hunting and primarily run jet boats for their operations. The Bighorn is very popular with local waterfowlers from Billings. Many of these guys have jet boats for hunting and fishing on the Yellowstone near home. Naturally, once the 'Stone is choked up with ice, they head to the Bighorn. So weekends and holidays can get crowded during duck season.

Prior to 1961, the Bighorn was a lazy, free-flowing river that tended to be warm, slow and full of silt. Catfish and carp were the primary fish species. The Yellowtail Dam changed all that. The dam turned the river into a cold, clear tailwater supporting healthy populations of brown and rainbow trout. Still, public access remained closed off by the Crow tribe. It took a landmark Supreme Court case in 1981, *Montana v. United States*, to change things. The court case held that the riverbed belonged to the State of Montana as a navigable waterway. Prior to that ruling, the tribe maintained sovereignty over the river. Those who risked hunting or fishing it, if caught, could be arrested at gunpoint. It was the arrest of a local fishing guide, Phil Gonzales, that led to the court's decision.[*]

An acquaintance once relayed a story to me about fishing the Bighorn when access was still forbidden. As he told me, in his mind, if no one is allowed to fish it, the fishing must be really good. He'd heard stories about anglers getting held up at gunpoint by tribal law enforcement, but that didn't stop him and his buddies. All was good and well until they floated around the bend in their rubber rafts and saw a group of what they thought was Crow law enforcement on horseback strung out across the river in a line, as if it was a blockade. They had time to row into a back eddy behind a wall of willows and figure out what they were going to do. In their minds, it was all about the river being closed to fishing, not floating. They figured if they just floated by and waved, with no fishing gear, they might just be allowed to pass. So they ditched their fishing gear on an island and headed downstream. As they neared the blockade, their worries dissipated as they

---

[*] Snow, "Godfather."

saw several of the horsemen were in the river, swimming and cooling off. On closer inspection, they realized it was just a bunch of cowhands taking a swim on their lunch break. They waved, smiled and floated on past without incident. He didn't mention if they came back for their fishing gear or not.

When hunters and anglers gained river access in 1981, the Bighorn became a highly sought-after fishing destination—and it still is. When it comes to waterfowl hunting, the Bighorn is a unique place, especially the colder it gets. With the dam keeping the water temperature constant, it stays open when air temps drop well below zero, becoming the only open water in a vast, frozen land. It's essentially a giant spring creek, and waterfowl leave area lakes and the Yellowstone River, all flocking to the Bighorn. Combine that with agriculture, which creates a ready-made food supply along the river corridor, and you have the makings for a perfect storm of ducks and geese.

This being a holiday weekend, word was that hunting pressure was thick on Saturday and Sunday. But the hunting was slow and tough, and most of the hunting traffic had dissipated by the time we arrived. When it comes to waterfowl hunting, though, sometimes serious hunting pressure can keep the birds moving, especially on public water. Duck hunting on the Bighorn is primarily a public access affair confined to the river. That day, there wasn't

Jet boats are a preferred method of travel on the Bighorn.

much to shoot at. However, we still had birds at drawn-out intervals passing by and giving us a look. The shots we ended up taking were longer than we'd have liked but still ethical. We'd have been better with it if they'd decoyed all the way in. We were waiting for "can't miss" shots over the decoys. Dale and I are waterfowl hunters of tradition, preferring ducks over decoys to anything else. We're in it for the dance, not the cake.

The country along the Bighorn is remote and unsettled compared to the riparian corridors of western Montana. There are no condos bunched up along the river, no cookie-cutter subdivisions, fancy restaurants, gas stations—nothing to mar the view or compete for water other than agriculture and a few rural residents. Of course, this benefits the river and its wildlife. The habitat is largely undisturbed save for the Yellowtail Dam, agriculture and the occasional home; outside the small town of Hardin and outpost of Fort Smith, it is wide-open country. Were it not Crow land, it might be a different story. The land can feel lonely and bleak in winter. Summer can get a bit insane with the fishing traffic, but come late-season waterfowl hunting, folks thin out considerably. Oh, there's still some hunting pressure. But it feels and looks like good hunting country: a healthy riparian corridor, agriculture that flows with the land, broken prairie above the river and the Bighorn mountains to the south. Best of all, damn few people. It's the way Montana is supposed to be.

Eventually, Dale and I had to admit our opportunities weren't going to get much better and we should take the next shots that presented themselves. The best opportunities we were going to get would be on the first pass, not the second or third, which most of the time never came. The next time a mallard drake passed overhead, Dale and I both fired. The bird fell to the ice on my left. Another came in not long after that, and I shot at him straight overhead. One shot dropped him into the decoys, ending in a big splash. This is a shot I don't prefer but Dale says is the easiest to connect on. He should know. He's competed in and taught shotgun marksmanship nearly as long as I've been alive.

As we entered into the final ten minutes of shooting time, the flight activity was picking up. Ducks would react to our spread and give us a good look but would never close. They'd keep on moving. We knocked down one more drake mallard before shooting time ended. Dale and I cleared our guns and told each other so. I walked over to where we'd stashed the ATV. This is when I saw the ducks and where they wanted to be. Looking out into the cornfield back toward the highway, I saw a swarm had materialized. Ducks in the hundreds, easily—probably over a thousand—were circling and

Late afternoon hunt, Bighorn River.

dropping into the corn. Scott had told us there were plenty of birds flying after shooting time. This was one of those sights you must stop and simply watch: the hundreds of black dots circling on the pink and purple horizon.

I told Dale what I'd seen when I pulled up to load our gear and head back to camp. He suggested maybe we hunt there tomorrow evening. I agreed it was a good plan. No wonder we couldn't get ducks to come into our decoys that day. When ducks want to be somewhere, it doesn't matter what you do.

We left the decoys out overnight and fell in on them the next morning. We didn't have a bird drop in all morning. I don't think we fired a shot. Three boats passed by headed back to Afterbay, all within an hour. It was probably nine thirty. We weren't the only ones feeling the slow hunting. Still, it was a beautiful morning, with the sunrise at our backs bringing warmth to the otherwise grim-looking cottonwoods along the river. About ten thirty or so, a fog drifted in from the north and shrouded everything around us. We hoped it would burn off before evening. It seemed an odd time for fog to move in, and for the moment, an eeriness came over the land.

Bighorn country has been wrapped in contention and haunting history for over a century. In 1876, George Armstrong Custer and Crow army scouts met their fate at the Battle of the Little Bighorn. From where Dale and I were hunting, the site of the battle is about forty miles away. Here, the Little Bighorn flows through a stretch of cottonwoods below a steep bench. It was on this bench country that the battle took place where Custer, the Seventh Cavalry and many Crow fell almost to a man at the hands of the Lakota Sioux, Northern Cheyenne and Arapaho tribes. This was and has always been Crow territory, and this was the primary reason they joined forces with the U.S. Army.[*]

Prior to westward expansion, Native tribes fought wars against each other over natural resources and territory—the same reasons wars are fought the world over. Warfare was also a cornerstone of many Native cultures. It was at this point in history that tribes like the Crow and Arikara could feel their grip slipping, as their populations had been decimated by years of disease epidemics and intertribal warfare. Without help, they were going to lose their land and identity at the hands of their enemies, the Sioux and Cheyenne. Their alliance with the United States embodied a last-ditch effort to save their people and their land.[†]

As a result, the Crow ended up with one of the largest reservations of all the Northern Plains Indian Tribes. Still, it's a fraction of what they got in the initial deal. They soon discovered the real price for their allegiance. As it did with many tribal treaties, the U.S. government incrementally made changes to the deal as it became apparent that prime ranching and mining country existed on Crow land. Piece by piece, portions were carved away. The railroad got its share as well: a four-hundred-foot right of way along the Yellowstone River corridor.[‡] In modern-day terms, a sovereign nation made the foreign policy decision to ally with another country in exchange for protection from greater threats, something that has been done the world over since time began. This set the stage for the tribal reservation system as it exists today. To be hunting amid this history is surreal and a little uneasy. I've had this feeling more than once afield contemplating the violent past in Montana's vast, quiet and lonely landscape.

Realizing the morning flight was over, we picked up dekes and went out to the field to scout a little. There was a remnant stand of cornstalks, which made an ideal blind. Partially eaten corncobs on the ground with kernels scattered around them indicated where the birds had been eating. Our setup was a no-brainer. We'd put the sun to our back and hunker down on stools in the cornstalks. After returning to camp for a midday break, our plan was to head to the cornfields around three o'clock. The fog burned off around one. The skies cleared and the sun shone bright. It was one

---

[*] Galloway, "Other Indians," 29.
[†] Galloway, "Other Indians," 40.
[‡] Galloway, "Other Indians," 40.

Dale Spartas settled into a Bighorn blind.

of those beautiful January afternoons that almost makes you forget about winter. We took a minimal decoy spread along, half a dozen with three spinners. The image of that duck vortex over the cornfield in my head made the anticipation palpable.

Dale and I sat ready as the sun began its incremental descent toward the Bighorns. It was probably 4:00 p.m. before we saw the first ducks on the move. Shooting time would end at 4:57. We had singles and groups of three to four circle and give us a look, much like they were doing on the river the day before. Then they'd move along. More ducks materialized along the river corridor, with a few peeling off to come check us out. They'd circle a time or two but keep going. What was the deal?! We had twenty minutes of shooting time left, and we were wondering how the ducks we saw yesterday were going to get here.

A flight of eight mallards circled us and looked very interested in dropping in. But they didn't. Soon I gave Dale the ten-minute warning. Then five minutes. More and more ducks began to build on the horizon near and far. They were circling now. One minute left to go and a lone mallard dropped down within range. I fired, and it folded. I then broke my gun and told Dale I was clear. But this wasn't over. Flight upon flight of ducks, mostly mallard, began to build overtop of us and prepare to land. It was like a switch flipped. They knew it was safe to land, and here they came. The first few birds touched down in the field one hundred yards out from us. With the ground team landed, ducks by the hundreds were now keyed in on them and built a cyclone of feathers over the field. Birds on the outer edge of the vortex would pass over, check out our dekes and then join the real ducks. Dale shouldered his unloaded shotgun and took practice swings on the decoying birds. I could hear him whispering to himself, "*Bang.*" Pause. "*Bang.*"

In the final moments of daylight on the closing day of the season, we just stood and watched what was probably over a thousand ducks cup and land all around us. We couldn't shoot, but we didn't care. Dale blew his hen call and watched their reactions. I couldn't think of a better way to end the season. Of course, a few mallards before shooting time ended would have been nice. But the sight of scores of ducks in a waning pink and purple sky is what warms a duck hunter's heart more than anything.

CHAPTER 10

A DUCK'S BEST FRIEND

I f you've ever wondered just what in the heck duck stamps do, exactly, you're about to find out. What does it take to keep ducks in the skies each fall? A lot of work by a lot of people. When you look at all that occurs daily to conserve waterfowl, at its core you will find a lot of dedicated, passionate people who never shirk the next waterfowl management challenge. Wildlife professionals toil over the course of a career, often never to realize the full impact of that career. Jim Hansen is one of those professionals who made a difference. If the definition of love is to will the good of the other, Jim loved ducks and duck hunters from the bottom of his heart.

It's difficult to imagine, given the seasons and duck populations hunters have known for the last twenty years, but the late 1980s and early '90s were a bleak time for ducks and duck hunting. Severe drought had dried up much of the Prairie Pothole Region (PPR). Hunting seasons had been cut drastically short, along with bag limits. Add to that a paradigm shift in shotgun ammunition from lead to nontoxic shot, and many were wondering if duck hunting was on the way out. There were a lot of folks who'd hung up their duck calls and shotguns. This is the duck-hunting landscape Jim found himself neck-deep in when he arrived in Montana with his family in 1991 to begin working as a waterfowl biologist with Montana Fish, Wildlife and Parks (FWP).

At about this same time, the Montana state duck stamp program, which began in 1986, began bringing extra funding, which—along with federal duck stamp funding and financial support from Ducks Unlimited—enabled much-needed habitat work. Jim already had twenty-five years of waterfowl management experience behind him when he arrived. He'd worked for the U.S. Fish and Wildlife Service and state agencies in Florida and the Midwest. He had experience working on the Mississippi Flyway Council and navigating the often-complex bureaucratic maze that entailed. Give him the resources, and he was off to the races with his paddle and boat cushion (more about that later).

When Jim began his Montana career, he got teamed up with FWP waterfowl biologist Jeff Herbert. Jeff had been in the saddle since the 1970s and saw waterfowl numbers plummet in the span of a few short years of serious drought conditions. It was at this same time that the Prairie Pothole Joint Venture (PPJV) formed to address the problems affecting ducks and their habitat. The PPJV was an agreement between northern- and southern-tier states in the Central and Mississippi Flyways to cooperatively manage northern breeding habitat. The ultimate goal was to boost waterfowl production, which affected turnout on wintering grounds down south.

Montana had areas in the northeastern part of the state where wetland densities were high and supported good duck production. Other areas had good grassland habitat for nesting cover but poor wetland density, which didn't produce ducks. Then there were areas where intense farming activity left little room for either. The goal Jim and Jeff were a big part of bringing forward was to get more water to those parts of the state that needed it and work with large private landowners to boost waterfowl production. But it was a hard sell to their bosses at the time. To them, it didn't make sense to focus on wetland habitat projects during a drought, especially in a state where big game gets the spotlight when it comes to wildlife management. In many people's eyes, waterfowl management was always something of a sideshow. Duck hunters weren't paying for a sideshow, though. The big challenge is that no state has its own waterfowl population. It's why the federal government has overarching management authority. Waterfowl migrate from the top to the bottom of the continent with unique habitat requirements throughout. Such species can't be managed in a decentralized fashion.

Jim and his colleagues worked on duck stamp–funded projects with a number of different stakeholders, from private landowners to other federal agencies, to get wetland projects underway, despite lots of questions from upper-level management. This involved developing impoundments, especially in areas of healthy grassland with little to no water. After years of persistent drought, moisture returned to the prairie, and ducks were everywhere! The North American Wetland Act Council would fly the prairie pothole region annually. When Jim, Jeff and their team toured Montana that year, their minds were blown. The landscape-scale effect of several years of impoundment work demonstrated why wetland enhancement was so critical for waterfowl populations. As Jeff described it: "It was like Shake 'n Bake ducks. All you need is ducks and water in the right place."

If it could be said that duck hunters had an advocate on two of the nation's flyway councils, Jim Hansen was it. While he started out in the Mississippi Flyway, Jim served most of his flyway council tenure on the Central Flyway, being in Billings. Each flyway council has a representative from each state and Canadian province, along with folks from the U.S. Fish and Wildlife Service. They hash out everything from season structures to bag limits and determine which species may need reduced or increased limits. Jim always advocated what was best for waterfowl populations. He always insisted that accurate and timely data got factored into management decisions.

Jim was one of the longest-serving members on the Central Flyway Council in his time. He began in his early forties and served until seventy-eight years of age, attending his last meeting from bed shortly before his death in 2022. Jim brought the perspective of time and experience to the council, helping inform many important decisions and regulation changes. Jim did not have patience for regulations that were arbitrary or didn't make sense. He always did what was best for the ducks, but he never believed in implementing regulations that made it hard for hunters to avoid mistakes.

Jim Hansen on a successful sandhill crane hunt near Harlowton. *Dennis Hagenston.*

When the season was closed on pintails, he advocated for the limit to be one bird, as a hen pintail could easily be confused with other species, especially early in the season. Jim, an avid hunter himself, knew how hard it could be to tell the difference between a hen pintail and a gadwall, of which there were plenty. At the same time, his review of the data trends told him that a one-bird limit on pintail would not have detrimental effects on the population.

Besides advocating for commonsense regulations on the flyway council, Jim also knew that hunters needed to be able to identify birds accurately in the field before shooting them. He was the best duck-hunting partner a waterfowler could hope for: easygoing, always charitable, quiet and unassuming. Waterfowl ID is probably the one thing that gets more duck hunters in trouble than anything else. It's just plain difficult—unless, of course, you were hunting with Jim Hansen. He pioneered duck identification classes in Montana and taught them for decades. Talk to his close hunting buddies, Dennis Hagenston and Roger Parker, and they'll tell you that with Jim in the blind, you never had to wonder what you were shooting at. If anyone could talk about the things that get duck hunters in trouble, these guys could. Dennis is a retired Montana game warden and Roger a retired federal game warden. Both spent decades enforcing the rules and regulations Jim and his colleagues on the flyway councils worked to develop.

Dennis recalls the exactness with which Jim could ID ducks on the wing in tough conditions.

"There's a lot of regulations to bear in mind, but when you've got the ducks screaming in from different directions, heights, light and weather, even when you think you know what duck it is, you may not. But Jim? He could tell you with certainty about 85 percent of the time. Jim and I were hunting up at Lake Mason near Roundup one time. We were hunting in ground blinds, which is a hard position to hunt from and hard to see, too. The light was poor. We'd take turns on incoming birds, and it was my turn. I saw what I thought was a gadwall. I swung on it and dropped it, then Jim says, 'Nice shot on that canvasback!'

"This other time, we were on the Bighorn. I had both my sons along. The season was closed on pintails. My son Art shoots a bird, and the dog is bringing it back, and I'm thinking, *That looks like a pintail*. Art hollers, 'Arrest me!' Jim glances at the bird from a distance and says, 'Hold on a minute. Let's take a look at that.' Turns out it was a mallard-pintail hybrid. Jim caught something about that instantly when he saw it. He's looked at so many ducks over the years, it just clicked in his brain automatically. Art thought he was shooting a mallard. So he brings it over to Jim. Jim starts pointing out the subtle details to us in the bill and the feet. I was focused on the feathers, which had pintail characteristics. So Jim says with a smile and his dry sense of humor, 'Well, in this case, I'd say its 51 percent mallard, 49 percent pintail, so I think you're legal.' I was glad I didn't have to write my own son a ticket!"

Roger, who has checked duck hunters from California to Alaska as a state and federal warden for thirty years, considers Jim to have been one of the most knowledgeable duck ID guys there was. "I always respected the knowledge Jim had. I've got a decent knowledge on waterfowl species and so forth, but Jim? I'm not even close to him. I'd always ask him questions, especially during early season when it's harder to tell between a bird of the year and other species. Jim would always clue me into the details that separated those birds. His knowledge on everything from bird diseases to species identification was unmatched."

The waterfowl identification class Jim started for hunters and the general public was a hallmark of his career. He also trained numerous state, federal and tribal game wardens in waterfowl ID. I once had the privilege of assisting Jim with one of his classes, and I can speak from firsthand experience: I've never seen anything like it. It was humbling to work with him. Jim loved working with people, especially those enthusiastic about waterfowl. With patience and gentleness, he would walk folks through the different aspects of waterfowl identification. He had amassed a wide-ranging collection of wings and stuffed ducks that participants could put their hands on. They could see, touch and feel in vivid detail what distinguished one duck species from another. Jim explained to them how to look at bird profiles, wing speculums, flight characteristics and size. He would also educate hunters and other folks about bird species often encountered in the same space as waterfowl. New and inexperienced hunters sometimes confuse other, non-huntable waterfowl species, such as grebes or cormorants, with legal species. Jim's waterfowl ID classes became quite popular over the years, and he never tired of the commitment. In addition to the classes, Jim was instrumental in Montana FWP's providing pocket-sized waterfowl ID guides with color plates to the public, free of charge.

Some folks come along at just the right time for the right reason. In Jim's case, his patience and people skills arrived right when Montana duck hunters needed them most. In 1991, nontoxic shot for waterfowl hunting became the law of the land. We take this for granted now: generations of duck hunters have known nothing else. But it's important to understand that at the time, this was a highly contentious issue. The federal government had stepped in to regulate ammunition for hunting. There had been some

Jim Hansen picking up decoys. Note the oar for balance. *Roger Parker.*

misinformation in the outdoor press at the time about steel shot's lethality as well as the reasons behind banning lead shot for waterfowl. During this time, a small cadre of outdoor writers held immense sway over waterfowl hunters' opinions, and what they said was gospel, even if their opinion wasn't fully informed. The joke at the time was: if you want to start a fight in less than five minutes, walk into a bar anywhere in Montana and mention steel shot. For many a duck hunter, this was a bitter pill.

It might have been easier had the difference between early steel and lead shot's lethality been marginal, but this wasn't the case. Lead could kill ducks at much greater distances than steel. It was denser and hit harder. However, it was also killing waterfowl in large numbers in certain places and not from a gun barrel—at least not directly. During the 1980s and even before that, scientific evidence had been accumulating that lead shot was killing waterfowl year-round. Being birds and having gizzards, waterfowl ingest small rocks and pebbles from wetland bottoms. Lead pellets were the perfect-sized pebble for that purpose. Once a pellet is ingested, lead poisoning ensues and kills the bird within a matter of days. In hunting areas where there was consistent hunting pressure on shallow lakes and marshes, lead shot accumulated in vast quantities. When ducks congregated on these wetlands in large numbers, mass die-offs occurred. While this didn't happen everywhere, it happened enough to begin causing serious concern. Soon the call for banning lead was being heard.

The big hurdle wildlife managers and the firearms industry had to clear was convincing hunters they could kill ducks with steel shot, which is still the most viable nontoxic option from an affordability standpoint. Jim was an advocate of the move to nontoxic shot, but he knew it would be a hard sell to hunters, being one himself. The challenge was to demystify the perceived less lethal nature of steel. Jim and Jeff organized shooting clinics every summer for several years where they would bring in famed ballistician Tom Roster, who'd done an amazing amount of work convincing bird hunters of steel shot's efficacy.

For several years, Jim and his colleagues would travel the state with Roster to put on shooting clinics and show hunters that steel shot did work. Everyone from sporting goods store owners to local waterfowl influencers were invited to these clinics. It took time, as there was a lot of misinformation to the effect that steel shot wouldn't kill birds effectively and that it would damage guns. The reality was that there was a learning curve. Hunters had to learn how steel shot performed differently. The bottom line was: if your shooting fundamentals were sound, there wasn't that much difference between lead and steel in your gun. Steel shot was hard on old shotgun barrels, but shot cup improvement helped this. Stories about steel shot ripping off the end of gun barrels were the kind of myths the shooting clinics helped disprove. True to form, Jim spent many a hot summer day at these shooting clinics inside a portable skeet house with plexiglass windows and not much ventilation to speak of. It never bothered him for a second.

Over time, acceptance of steel shot among Montana waterfowlers took hold. But it wasn't by accident. Persistent and diligent work by wildlife professionals and conservation-oriented hunters led the effort to fruition. To this day, the Tom Roster nontoxic shot lethality tables are still published in the Montana waterfowl regulations every season. These tables break down shot sizes appropriate for the type of waterfowl you are hunting, as well as range capabilities of nontoxic ammunition.

What's important to remember is that while Jim Hansen was a dedicated biologist, he was also an avid hunter. He loved this resource with every fiber of his being. Knowing Jim the duck hunter is every bit as important as knowing Jim the scientist. Like all good, experienced duck hunters, Jim had his habits and eccentricities. Such habits and eccentricities are part of the fun duck hunters engage in, especially with partners who do things more conventionally. When retired federal warden Roger Parker and Jim first started hunting together, there were the usual discussions about decoys: how many to bring and who would bring what. Roger wasn't a decoy baron by any stretch, only possessing about two to three dozen—which, for duck hunters in the know, isn't that many.

Jim told Roger not to worry about decoys. He would bring his. When they got to the duck hole, Roger asked Jim how many decoys they would put out. Jim responded matter-of-factly, "Oh, about six or eight." He was a man of simplicity. He didn't worry about the latest and greatest gear. He always showed up on a hunt wearing a green army jacket with the same canvas duffle of gear, a handful of decoys, a boat cushion and a paddle. Jim and retired Montana game warden Dennis Hagenston would walk in more than a mile to their spots sometimes. As they hunted the prairie a lot, cover was always scarce. Jim typically packed along a bundle of willow twigs to fashion a quick, basic blind. He never brought along anything prefab.

His boat cushion and paddle were two things Jim never went anywhere without. They became trademarks of his, at work or play. People would always ask why he had them. "You never know when you might need them," Jim would say. He'd use the paddle for a walking stick wading through the marsh to hunt or to gauge water levels on a habitat project. In later years, it kept him upright in the muck when picking up decoys. Whatever the situation, the paddle was always handy. As for the boat cushion, he always had a flotation device close at hand while on or near water. It also kept his backside comfortable and warm in the field. The older Jim got, the more he seemed to delight in carrying these things. It added an air of professorial eccentricity with young colleagues, who wondered why this old guy was always packing around an oar and a boat cushion.

Megan O'Reilly, a nongame biologist and protégé of Jim's who worked with him in the latter part of his career, always scratched her head at Jim's accoutrements—until one day, she found herself out in a boat at work alone without a paddle and needing to balance herself. In that moment, she thought, *Man, I wish I had Jim's paddle.* She inherited the paddle following Jim's passing.

Jim, Dennis and Roger all seemed to hit their stride in the sportsman stage of hunter development about the same time. None cared about shooting a limit—or anything at all, for that matter. Quite often, regardless of what the legal limit was, they'd come up with their own limit for the day, which was often a bird or two less than what was legally allowed. They also took turns taking shots, to the point where only one of them shot at a time. It's a special group of waterfowlers who can engage in such restraint.

Jim Hansen and Fancy. *Roger Parker.*

They had a spot they hunted south of Billings for years. It was a warm spring slough Jim had discovered in the course of his work. He developed a good relationship with the landowner and as a result, along with Dennis and Roger, experienced many good hunts there over the years. At any good hunting spot, there are lots of good days, and then there's a small handful of exceptional days. One of those exceptional days occurred late one December. No open water existed in the area except for the spring slough they were hunting. From the initial wave of ducks, they had cut out a bird or two each. Then the mallards came, wave after wave, bright greenheads cupping and dropping into the slough. Behind the decoying birds were faint specks on the horizon, getting larger and larger as they neared the water. Wave after wave kept coming. All agreed it was the most magnificent sight they'd ever seen. They unloaded their guns, sat back and just watched. The dogs had quizzical looks on their faces, but the hunters didn't care. Each of them had labored their entire professional lives to make moments like this possible. They knew it was special and just wanted to enjoy the moment.

If Jim had a soft spot, it was his dogs: black Labs, to be exact. Jim loved them all dearly. He worked and trained them accordingly. Jim's longtime colleague and hunting companion Jeff Herbert once said, "Most of Jim's dog training occurred in the rocking chair with the dog on his lap." None of Jim's approaches to dog handling would be found in a book on retriever training. But in Jim's case, it worked. And he was OK with it. His dogs were family members first and foremost. He might do some bumper throws occasionally, but when retrieves got challenging, Jim reached into his pack and pulled out a cigar box. Inside, the box was partitioned off: one side for cigars, the other for a collection of small rocks. Jim fondly called these rocks "retriever helper." If one of his dogs was not marking a bird well, Jim would toss the rocks in the bird's direction until the dog zeroed in. Jeff, who trained his Labs religiously in conventional retriever fashion, would get exasperated and say, "Jim, there's better ways to do this!" Jim would just shrug, grab another rock and toss it out there.

Jim didn't like his dogs to be uncomfortable. His last Lab, Fancy, always got the royal treatment, seated next to Jim in the blind wrapped in a blanket with an outer layer of burlap for camo. If rain or snow was in the forecast, she'd have a tarp covering her with just her head poking out. If a person got asked, "What kind of animal would you want to be?" an intelligent response would be: "One of Jim Hansen's Labs."

Jim was a gentleman sportsman of the finest sort. He dedicated his life to waterfowl conservation as a wildlife biologist, but he came to enjoy and care about waterfowl on a deeply personal level. When hunting, Jim was there for the experience, to relax and get away from it all. A duck season or two before Jim's death, Roger Parker recalls how relaxed and at peace Jim was in the blind. They were on a goose hunt near Hysham along the Yellowstone River. It had been a slow start to the morning. Then, eventually, a couple of geese came in. Roger shot, knocking one down. Jim's gun remained silent. Then his voice piped up. "Did you get one?! Holy cow, I fell asleep!"

Jim Hansen passed away on October 1, 2022, on opening day of Montana's waterfowl season. The time was noon, about when Jim would have normally come in from hunting. In the latter years of his career, Jim had worked to help the U.S. Fish and Wildlife Service acquire a 2,766-acre piece of waterfowl habitat near Grass Lake National Wildlife Refuge and adjacent to Big Lake Wildlife Management Area northwest of Billings. Established as a federal Waterfowl Production Area, it boasts 1,850 wetland acres and expanded the area's waterfowl habitat to be held in the public trust. Jim had discovered the area during his habitat work and hunted there on occasion. In a fitting tribute to his lifelong dedication to waterfowl conservation, it was designated the James L. Hansen Waterfowl Production Area.

Central Flyway Council

Alberta   Kansas   Nebraska   North Dakota   Oklahoma   South Dakota   Wyoming
Colorado   Montana   New Mexico   Northwest Territories   Saskatchewan   Texas

https://centralflyway.org

September 16, 2022

Jim Hansen
1308 Steffanich Drive
Billings, MT 59105

Dear Jim:

The Central Flyway Council, Technical Staff, and Committee membership would like to recognize you for your tireless service, leadership, mentoring, professional expertise, and personal friendship that you have shared for over 32 years on the Central Flyway and another 10 years on the Mississippi Flyway. Our collective relationship resembles a close-knit family, and you have graciously lent your time to the least of us without fail. You remain an example for biologists and leaders throughout our profession.

Through your entire career, you have served as a shining example. You have improved wetlands through habitat projects; improved management of migratory game birds, migratory shore birds, passerine birds, and other species; fostered good relations among multiple states and the US Fish and Wildlife Service; contributed to training biologists; and participated in public education. And that is just for starters! Your longstanding and consistence service has added stability and institutional knowledge for Montana and for the entire Central Flyway. The frequency with which you make personal trips to examine water levels, migratory status of waterfowl, fence line maintenance, livestock access, delivery of banding materials, and provide educational opportunities is legendary. Tirelessly, you coordinate among the myriad agencies and volunteers to ensure our monitoring meets quality standards. Although turnover and churn are common terms in our profession, your steadfast performance and approach to management have served to add stability to the work to which we all contribute.

Your professional contributions are seemingly countless, yet more notable to those of us that have grown to know you is the personal touch you add to the professional relationships we share. Few among us lack a personal anecdote that includes how you reached out to include an individual in a learning opportunity, how you mentored another biologist through difficult decisions or negotiations, how you truly listened to the public and responded to their requests, how you engaged in watching and pursuing our precious wildlife resources with others, or how you fostered lasting friendships!

Central Flyway Council's letter to Jim Hansen upon his retirement, page 1. *Phyllis Hansen.*

You have added richness to our lives, and we are grateful for your professional and personal contributions.

With sincere friendship:

Jim,
Thanks For all for you have done for The birds. Tom Cooper

Jim
Thank you for your dedication to waterfowl.
Casey Anderson

Jim—
Thank you for all you have done for Waterfowl and your dedication to the resource! Best Angi Bruce

Jim,
thank you for teaching us how to find our way thru the sticker bushes. — Rocco

JIM, Thanks For all your work and assistance for us CFT MT!

Jim,
Thank you for your many years of service!!
John W. Deasy

Jim,
Thank you for your lifetime of dedication & service. Best, Jerry Blew

Jim,
Thank you for being such a great mentor!
—Alicia Hardin

Jim
Thank you for your knowledge & passion it has been a pleasure it has been a pleasure to work with you the last decade. I only hope we have more like you in the Future!
Shaun

Jim,
Thank you for all your hard work ensuring the future of Waterfowl! It has been a pleasure working with you.
Stewart

Jim, this letter says it far better than I could. It has been my privilege to serve with you the many years. Thank you for all you've done for the resource and our profession.

Central Flyway Council's letter to Jim Hansen upon his retirement, page 2. *Phyllis Hansen.*

11/30/96

Dear Mr. Hansen,

Thanks a million for the great experiences duck hunting! I really enjoyed it and I'm sure I'll enjoy hunting them for years to come. I really needed that spark that you gave me to start my duck hunting obsession. Before then I was confined with no knowledge of ducks and duck hunting. I had no idea of the thrill when a mallard or wood duck or any other duck drops into the decoys in front of you. It is just that feeling that you fooled those ducks into comming down it is like no other sensation in the world. I can't even begin to thank you enough for the outings and experiences. I really appreciated it and hope maybe we can do it again sometime. Thanks!

Your Friend
Jay

P.S. Thanks for the pictures they're "superb". Also your ducks in the other "article" I really enjoyed it. I also enjoyed your article. "Lowel Washburns article" Sandy

Letter to Jim Hansen from a young duck hunter he mentored. *Phyllis Hansen.*

POSTSCRIPT: I owe a deep debt of gratitude to Jim's wife, Phyllis Hansen. It is because of her time, insight and willingness to share that I was able to piece together Jim's network of friends, colleagues and experiences. Like many spouses of career-focused individuals, Phyllis married not only Jim but also his career as a wildlife biologist. It is a special spouse who loves and supports that person through all the ups, downs, joys and sorrows of an impactful career. Jim's story is her story, and she tells it with enthusiasm, dry wit and honesty.

CHAPTER 11

HI-LINE SAFARI

Thousands of ducks. That's what I saw. As I swept the vast expanse of Lake Bowdoin with my binoculars, the entire surface appeared covered with waterfowl. And water. This year, the balance sheet got a good adjustment from the last three years of drought. Winter snowpack had been generous, too. Looking at the SNOTEL map back in March, I remember being a little shocked when I saw the Milk River drainage at 250 percent of average. This was the highest in the state, perhaps anywhere in the West. All the potholes were full, along with the bigger water. The refuges, waterfowl production areas, wildlife management areas: everything was looking up. This time last year, there was hardly a duck or water to speak of in this country.

I traveled 320 miles from my home in southwest Montana, the better part of a day, to get to the Hi-Line. Turning east at Malta, I now had to sort out hunting it. Montana's Hi-Line was originally the main line of the Great Northern Railway, the northernmost transcontinental railroad line in the United States—thus its name. "Hi-Line" also refers to US Highway 2, which parallels the railroad and the northern tier of Montana that borders the Canadian provinces of Saskatchewan and Alberta. Pick whichever line works, but once you're up here, the name makes all the sense in the world. It's wide, vast country stretching from the Rocky Mountain front to the North Dakota line. As one travels east along the Hi-Line, one enters the western end of the continent's duck breadbasket, called the Prairie Pothole Region.

The land rolls and breaks, revealing small and large divots in the prairie, which in good years hold water and create habitat ideal for waterfowl production. There is the mistaken notion that eastern Montana is flat as a pancake from top to bottom. Nothing could be further from the truth. Anyone who explores the depths of the area never thinks or says that again. At a glance, it may appear flat. But you can't travel far without glimpsing of one of several island mountain ranges that break the horizon: the Little Rockies, the Bear's Paw, the Sweet Grass Hills. These and other sentinels that dot the prairie will at some point be in view of any traveler to the Hi-Line.

Rivers like the Milk, Marias and Missouri contain a world all their own, not visible until you are upon them. Along their courses run flats of cottonwood and willow that create an oasis for wildlife tucked below the vast expanse of prairie. In fall, these riparian zones appear as arteries of golden lifeblood flowing through the stark, tanned grasses and blue-gray expanse of sagebrush. When you're down at water's edge in these places, you could mistake them for somewhere in the southeast or the Midwest—for a minute or two.

I'd always wanted to explore and hunt this country. I'd made shorter, focused trips here for big game. But that confines you to a small area. I wanted to roam this country and take in its breadth. It's a wide, vast landscape that in the right years is abundant with ducks. In the wrong years, it is desolate, dry and seemingly devoid of life. Seldom are things in balance, if ever, on this land. This year was bountiful. At every turn, it was loaded with water and ducks.

The plan was to be mobile and hunt from east to west in safari fashion. I towed my light, enclosed utility trailer, which would serve as camp and additional gear storage. Hunting gear was in the bed of my pickup, with a canoe strapped to the roof. I'd done a fair amount of map reconnoiter and centered in on several areas between Malta and Havre. With ten days in the bank, I'd spend two days in one area, then move on to the next. The plan was to hunt a different spot each day on public land and scout tomorrow's in the afternoon. It was going to be an interesting hunt.

Lightning flashed in the skylight of the trailer. Thunder rumbled gently to the south. Rain fell lightly on the roof at four thirty in the morning. It was opening day, and I was hunting Bowdoin National Wildlife Refuge. In the morning darkness, I could hear thousands of ducks out on the lake: mallard, wigeon, teal. With decoys and gear loaded in the sled, I trudged off toward the water's edge and hoped for the best. The unknown factor was the depth of the water and mud between me and the small nesting island I was going to hunt from. I left the grass and walked over a crusted mudflat. Soon my boots busted through, and I could feel the thickening pull of prairie mud. Hitting the water, the mud seemed to lessen. I got a steady walk going and could see the silhouette of the island dead ahead. Arriving at the island, I got to work pitching decoys from my Texas rig system. I'd converted over to this at the insistence of some friends last season. Your decoy lines are loose and hooked to a carabiner. The weight slides up and down the line. They untangle fast and pick up fast. It saves a lot of time. After pitching out eighteen blocks, I deployed the jerk string, then settled into my layout blind to await legal shooting time.

Lightning streaked across the sky to the southwest over the Little Rockies. Thunder was way off. I couldn't remember if I'd ever started a duck hunt with thunder and lightning. Rain was due to pick up not long after daylight. As gray light crept in, birds were on the move. Morning flyout at Bowdoin had begun. Soon, hundreds, then thousands of ducks were in the skies. This was why I was here. To watch their dark silhouettes fill the empty gray space of sky gladdens the soul. Wind picked up from the east, and birds came in low toward the decoys. Legal shooting time had arrived.

I heard shotguns thump to the south of me but nothing close. I wasn't in a hurry to start shooting; several birds gave me passing shots I let go. The daily limit was six ducks, with individual species restrictions: one pintail this year, for instance. The possession limit was three times the daily limit. I would be hunting for ten days. I planned to eat ducks as I went, but still, I couldn't eat a limit every day—unless it was all teal, maybe. So I decided to shoot no more than three or four birds a day. Those would get cooked and consumed nightly or spread out between lunch and dinner. If the number of birds around was any indication, I'd stay well fed.

A lone green-wing came into the decoys, and I folded him on the first shot. First duck of the trip. Green-wings are always a mainstay of the bag in Montana, and I love the little guys. The first wave of rain came through and was fairly robust. Wind had been out of the southwest all morning, then shifted to the northeast. First front of the trip. I shot two more teal, a green-wing and a blue-wing. My shots that morning were all passing, not much decoying.

An interesting discovery in daylight was my hunting spot being covered in duck feces. I'm not talking about a little, either. It was everywhere. In one sense, that means you're in the right spot. In another sense, if any bird disease transmitted by fecal matter is going to cross the species barrier, this

Mobile prairie duck camp.

would be the place for it to happen. Gear would need a good cleaning back in camp. The more I looked at the soil on this island, the more it appeared that the island could be a giant pile of duck poop.

A wigeon decoyed out to my right, and I collected him with two shots. It was a little before ten o'clock, and I now had four birds to bag. I finished off the last of my thermos of coffee and daily ration of my wife's homemade banana bread. Back at the truck, I drove the south side of the refuge to take a look at where I might hunt tomorrow and see what hunting pressure was like. I counted three other vehicles in the entirety of the refuge besides myself. In effect, there was no real hunting pressure at all. I found a spot on the south end of the refuge where the water was deeper and amenable to launching a canoe. There were plenty of ducks rafted up nearby and not a soul around.

I headed back to camp and cooked some of last year's duck in celebration of the opener, with a side of wild rice. Ben, the local game warden, stopped by to say hi, and we visited for about an hour. While the rain had ceased, the wind was picking up significantly. With temps in the fifties, I staked out the ground blind and waders to dry off in the wind. I got my kill from the morning plucked and in the cooler. Surprisingly, the birds were already packing on some fat. A lot of guys like to breast ducks out to save time, but if birds have fat on them, it's criminal not to leave the skin on and do the extra work of plucking. With a layer of fat, the seasoning work is already done. Duck breast and leg held together with fat-laden skin, grilled quickly and not overdone, needs almost no seasoning at all. A touch of salt and pepper and it's as savory as a ribeye, in my opinion.

The following morning, I launched the canoe on the south end of the refuge and had another good hunt, bringing in four ducks: one green-winged and one blue-winged teal, one mature mallard drake and a wigeon. The wind blew steady all morning, and I was close to a busy rail line: six trains must have passed by during the hunt. The canoe was essential as it opened up a lot more options on these sprawling prairie lakes. No matter where the ducks were, I could get to them, long as I didn't mind paddling. In truth, I quite enjoyed it.

Two days into the trip, it was time to move camp and search out other areas to hunt. I had my eye on waterfowl production areas (WPAs) farther north. There was a sizeable lake along with some oxbow sloughs just off the Milk River. Arriving in the area, I found another piece of state land adjacent to the WPA where I could drop camp. Rain had been intermittent all morning. A fine mist was sifting down, giving the landscape a damp hue. I could see ducks all over the lake through binoculars. There was a prominent point they favored on the north shore. The water was perfect canoe depth and flush at the shorelines, no mudflats anywhere. The prairie rolled down to the water's edge. The point had dispersed patches of tule and cattail around it, which would make for good cover. I spent the rest of the afternoon scouting area WPAs and wildlife management areas.

I dropped off the prairie into the river bottoms along the Milk. With the light mist, cool temps and fall colors, I was reminded of my old duck haunts down south in late November. Things are always a couple of months ahead north of the forty-fifth parallel. This area of the WPA complex is walk-in only, with no boat launches, so I took off on foot toward some sloughs to see what the duck situation was. I decided to take a look at an oxbow just across the road from the parking area. Easing up under the cottonwoods, I heard wood ducks squealing softly. I couldn't see them, as the slough was lined with cattails eight to ten feet high. However, the banks sloped steeply to the slough, giving me a vantage over it. I could see a pair of woodies swimming along the edge of the cattails. It wasn't that far from the truck to drag the canoe and ease it down the hill to the water. Perhaps tomorrow afternoon I'd float it for a jump shoot.

Ducks flock to Bowdoin National Wildlife Refuge in fall.

The next morning dawned foggy with low-hanging clouds. No rain. From camp, I could hear duck racket out on the lake: hen mallards, wigeon whistles and the low grunting of coots. Decoys loaded in the canoe, I paddled toward the point I'd seen the ducks rafted up near. There was a slight headwind but nothing unmanageable. The canoe glided across the lake surface. A canoe makes hauling gear to the blind a breeze. It also enables you to retrieve birds in deeper water if you don't have a dog. Just paddling a canoe to the duck blind in the dark is fun.

Dekes out, I set my layout blind in knee-high alkali grass where it met tules. The skies remained the same dull gray as the last two days. No lightning or thunder that morning. The front that had been passing through the last couple of days seemed to be wrapping up. A steady north wind blew, with temps in the lower forties. The skies were due to clear up midday. There was a nice open stretch of water twenty yards wide to my front that met another band of tules out in the lake. This gave me a perfect gauge of when to shoot at birds. If they were past that outer band of tules, they were too far.

The morning flyout began. Not as many birds as I'd seen at Bowdoin, but we're still talking thousands on the wing. A flight of pintail jetted by at the outer edge of the tules before I was ready. No birds seemed to want to decoy, so it was shaping up to be a pass shooting day. A flight of gadwall came in, and I folded a hen out of the bunch. I saw lots of teal on the wing that morning, nearly all of them blue-wings. They almost fooled me for gadwalls with their white speculum feathers. Their smaller size gives them away. The clouds were beginning to break up, and I could see a faint hint of blue sky.

Shooting drakes only is a noble goal among waterfowlers, and one I strive for as much as possible. That far north and that early in the season, it can be tough. There are many ducks still in eclipse plumage, and young drakes of the year are often indistinguishable from a hen in flight. Sex ID is practically impossible in some cases. This is where it also pays to be mindful of regulations. With mallards, only two hens are allowed. Pintails: only one, period, regardless of sex. Pintails can usually be distinguished by their long, graceful necks. They also have an overall slim appearance compared to gadwalls or mallards.

Then you get into your divers: that season, it was two redheads and two canvasbacks per day. Divers have distinctive flight patterns compared to puddle ducks and, with practice, can be easy enough to sort out. It's key to let ducks get as close as possible before shooting. Watch how they fly, listen to their calls, look for certain colors. Also, waiting a little past legal shooting time can help a lot, as it can be very difficult to distinguish species when all you have to go by is the black silhouette of a duck. I'm saying this because I've shot more than a few hens in low-light conditions.

Duck ID is detail oriented.

At five birds, I was done for the morning. Clouds were breaking up, and sunlight was starting to bathe the hills. I picked up dekes, slipped the canoe into the lake and headed toward camp. I'd grill up the ducks marinating in the cooler and prep today's take for lunch tomorrow. Thus far, my diet had been ducks, and that's as it should be on a duck safari. After lunch, I took in a short nap, which had been much needed. The afternoon was warm and pleasant as the clouds dissipated and blue sky took over. With the afternoon free, I headed down into the Milk River plain with plans to stalk wood ducks in the oxbow I'd scouted yesterday.

Coming off the high prairie down along the river brought with it stark contrasts. For starters, it had warmed up enough to wake every dormant mosquito in the area. Bug dope applied, I loaded the shotgun, dry bags and camera gear into the canoe and portaged two hundred yards to the edge of the oxbow I'd seen wood ducks in yesterday. I eased the canoe down the steep embankment to the wall of eight-foot-high cattails at the bottom where the slough began. One foot in the canoe and one foot on the bank, I pushed forward, breaching the jungle wall of cattail, then glided out into the slough. No wood ducks flushed at my arrival.

Resting the shotgun on the canoe's thwart, I paddled slowly along the edge of the cattails. This was going to be a bit tricky, as I'd have the paddle in hand and need to get to the shotgun in time to make a decent shot on flushing woodies. To do this most effectively, I paddled on my knees to make a lower profile. I'd paddle a few strokes and let the canoe just glide along. The wood ducks would swim in and out of the cattails, so they could be anywhere along the slough. The cattails begin to tighten up, and I was paddling a narrow channel that twisted and turned. I marveled at the contrast in landscapes from that morning until now. Beginning the morning on a wide-open prairie lake, I now found myself in the depths of a riverine jungle. I'd expected a lot in advance of this trip. This I had not. The Hi-Line holds many surprises.

As I came into an open stretch of the slough, two wood ducks flushed at the far end, well out of range. This was going to be a lot tougher than I thought. I paddled to where they flushed and the slough necked down to a jungle of cattail. As I maneuvered the canoe into the narrow channel, paddle in hand, two drake woodies flushed at ten yards right in front of me, feet away. This oxbow slough kept going. I paddled through more cattail jungle in hopes of scoring on a woodie or two. The daily limit was only three. I took a long shot on a pair of flushing woodies and missed. As I turned around and began working my way back, a woodie flushed from the depths of the cattails behind me. They seemed to be everywhere

The Texas rig decoy system streamlines putting out and picking up.

when I was paddling and nowhere when I was holding a shotgun. Still, as I pulled up to the edge of the slough where I'd slipped in two hours ago, I couldn't have felt more satisfied with the action and variety of hunting I'd packed into a day.

Leaving the Malta country behind, I headed for water north of Chinook. Turning north at Zurich, I climbed toward the border to scope out several reservoirs and wetlands I'd seen on the map. The water I did find looked good and had a few ducks on it but not the numbers for a good hunt. The problem a duck hunter will run into out there is one of size. Those little potholes can be very enticing in appearance. They look real ducky. However, after the first shots are fired, ducks will simply fly to the next one—which could be five to ten miles away—where nobody is shooting at them. Your hunt is over at that point. I needed good-sized water where a large number of birds wanted to be.

The ducks appeared more dispersed in this country, and finding large concentrations was proving tough. I turned west by an old ranch house and began following a dirt two-track along a power line. In wet conditions, this road would have been impassable: the fresh ruts from rains only a few days ago demonstrated this. Fortunately, most of the ground was dry. I came upon a small wetland, off which about twenty mallards took to the sky. At the same time my truck passed in full view and spooked the birds, a coyote shot out from a patch of sagebrush, high-tailing it south. Many a coyote is shot from a pickup in this country. I'd interrupted his hunting plans.

I had one last spot to check before dark. It was the biggest patch of water in the area. If there weren't ducks here, any plans to hunt the Chinook country would have to be reconsidered. I had roughly an hour until dark and no spot to hunt yet. The reservoir I was headed toward was surrounded by BLM land, so I could camp there if needed. I turned from the improved gravel I was on onto a dirt two-track. I could see pieces of the reservoir across the mostly flat terrain. Sweeping it with the glass, I found it covered in ducks. Covered! I could hear the cacophony of sounds from the truck.

I had probably thirty minutes of daylight left as the sun sank to the west. So I decided to take a walk and see if I could find a good spot for a blind. Getting nearer the water, I could hear every duck call imaginable: pintail and wigeon whistling, gadwall humming, teal hen shrieks and, of course, mallards quacking. I found a seat on a rock under a Russian olive and took in the scene. The sky was fading orange with the sun gone. Ducks took flight, forms stark in the fading light.

Considering the sun direction tomorrow, I walked farther along the dike, where I found a patch of willows that provided good cover. Water was about twenty yards in front. I couldn't have hoped for a better turn of events at last light. Despite the sparse country, I'd found the ducks and a good spot for a blind. Anticipation ran high as I walked back to the truck and set up camp for the night.

The weather trended in a stable, mild direction. Lows would be crisp at around thirty-four degrees, but the next several days showed highs in the mid-seventies, clear and sunny. I heated a pot of red beans and rice on the camp stove. The stars were thick and brilliant as the moon wasn't up yet. The marsh chorus kept up on the lake, momentarily drowned out by several coyote packs chatting about a night's hunting. I soaked up every ounce of these gentle fall evenings in camp as I did mornings in the marsh.

Arising before the alarm became a trend over the course of this trip—a good thing! It was a crisp thirty-two degrees the next morning, with no wind. I got a little off course on the walk in and spooked some mallards off a small pothole not far from camp. I was at the blind around six, which gave me good time to set up. With no wind, I put the jerk string out and two pods of decoys left and right of the blind. I settled in among the willows, shotgun and shells prepped, then poured fresh coffee from the thermos. Sipping hot coffee in the twilight before legal shooting time is half the reason I go duck hunting in the first place. Ducks took wing out front, and

I could see small flights on the horizon. The crisp air, the smell of coffee wafting into my nostrils and dawn breaking at my back… It was a good day already.

The first duck of the morning to come in close was a drake pintail. I could see the soft tones of his gray, white and burgundy head plumage in the warm morning light. He had a long tail sprig to boot. As he cupped and came closer, I took my first shots of the morning. I missed both times, and he flew away unscathed. That was a heartbreak.

Ducks on the wing grew in number, and I could see flights of mallard reducing air speed up high, showing interest in my decoys. The sun rose, bathing the Bear's Paw Mountains to the south in soft orange light. Teal were everywhere. I couldn't keep them out of the decoys. Having shot a fair number this week, I was letting them pass, as I wanted to bring home some big ducks today. I had several groups of mallard circle and hit the brakes. The first rays of sun accenting mallard drakes in flight is one of those quintessential scenes in waterfowling. It has been captured so many times in waterfowling art. Nothing touches seeing it in real time. It is nostalgic and mesmerizing.

A small sled is indispensable for hauling gear across the prairie.

The next flight of teal that came in, I collected a couple. I'm glad I did, too, as I was not doing so hot with my shooting that morning. Then I took a drake mallard decoying in. One more teal and that was it for the day. I could have filled the limit with teal but held off. They were flying in and out of the decoys nonstop all morning. About ten thirty, the flying really slowed down. Still, it had been a phenomenal morning. Everything had an air of perfection about it. The warm, angular fall light; ducks of all stripes on the wing; the cool, crisp morning: it felt perfect. It reminded me of those youthful moments that hooked me on duck hunting in the first place.

Every hunting trip should have a good arc to it. Things start out good, you get into a good rhythm, there are some unexpected turns along the way, but things work out and the unexpected turns become good memories. As you clear the arc and things move toward the end, you want a good conclusion, a good note. Hunting is always uncertain, but before the inevitable drive home begins, you want to have that last good day that makes the arc, the journey, complete and a feeling of: *Oh yeah, that was worth it.*

With one hunt left to go, I'd reached the point where all my options had played out. Spots that should have water and ducks seemed to be drying up—literally, in most cases. As luck would have it, I came into Havre Sunday afternoon and had to stop at the hunter check station there. One of my fellow wardens, Andy, was working. After he checked my ducks and licenses, we discussed what might be some good options for my last day. There was Fresno Reservoir just outside of Havre, which is the biggest body of water in the area. There were sure to be ducks there. Then Andy told me about a spot west of there that he'd passed by the other day while on patrol. He said it was full of ducks. That was all I needed to hear. I thanked him and hit the road.

Headed west out of Havre, I turned north on yet another gravel road. As I drove toward Canada again, the Sweet Grass Hills came into view to the west. About fifty miles off, from atop those prairie sentinels, the Rocky Mountain Front comes into view. Grizzly bears have occasionally shown up and snagged a cow for dinner coming off the Marias River in search of food. I had traveled far on this trip.

The lake revealed itself as I came over a slight rise in the prairie. It was wide enough and arced back into the folds of the prairie, telling me I could see only a small portion of it. The surface was covered with water parsnip. The lake straddled either side of the road, and I could see large numbers of ducks rafted up in both directions. Sweeping it with binoculars, then pulling out the spotting scope, I saw all the usual puddler suspects. More intriguing were the numbers of divers I saw out in deeper water: redhead, scaup, maybe a canvasback or two. I watched flights of them coming in hot with their feet down and angled out in diver fashion. All along the edges of the lake in shallower water, I saw ducks loafing in the warm, gentle afternoon sun. The hunt would end here.

Bureau of Reclamation land surrounded the lake, so I could camp anywhere I could park. I found the perfect spot to back in and drop the trailer only fifty yards from the lakeshore. The afternoon was warm and pleasant, in the high seventies. I was in a thin shirt, light pants and Crocs. Indian summer is a beautiful thing. The plan was simple, and I'd been waiting to do this all trip: launch the canoe, decoys and all, make a good waterborne reconnoiter of the lake, pick a spot for the morning, put out decoys, set up the layout blind and be ready to go for tomorrow morning.

Paddling the lakeshore farther in, I kept jumping wad after wad of ducks at water's edge. The lake got deep quick, within ten yards of the shore in most places. I was hoping to find a spot where the sun would be at my back in the morning, but that wasn't working out the way the lake sat. I would have to settle for it coming in from the side. I pitched the puddler dekes in the shallows and then the diver string with a ball of dekes at one end farther out. I brushed the layout blind with alkali grass against a short wall of Canadian thistle, which helped with cover. I guess noxious weeds are good for something, although I didn't appreciate the numerous stickers and seed pods on my shirt sleeves and pants.

With the whole setup ready for the morning, I paddled back to camp, soaking in the last of the gentle fall light and pleasant warm air. The paddle back took about twenty minutes—not bad. Kicking back in camp, I sipped a cold beer and listened to the sounds of the marsh in the still, gentle fall evening. It is a sound I shall miss. The quack-and-whistle language of ducks, the splashing and grunting of coots, air rushing through wings overhead. There was also the smell of the marsh. Dead, decaying vegetation, wet alkali mud: that wet, muddy smell ties it all together.

The last morning began clear, calm and cool, about forty-six degrees. In the moonlight, I launched the canoe and began paddling toward the blind. Stars twinkled in the half moonlight that bathed the prairie and the lake surface. Nothing beats paddling a canoe to a duck blind on still water. Unlike in moving water, where you're constantly minding your course and watching out for hazards, you can take things in. I paddled a stroke here and there and kept the canoe easing forward while listening to the sounds of a marsh still on night shift.

Arriving at the blind, I stashed the canoe against a line of Canadian thistle and stretched the camo net over it. I double-checked the inside of the layout blind with a light before settling in. The prairie rolled right down to the water's edge, and it had been a warm day yesterday; I didn't want to share my duck blind with a rattlesnake. All clear, I slipped in and readied my gear for the morning. Dawn began with that long, thin sliver of light across the eastern prairie horizon. Ducks were on the move fifteen minutes prior to shooting time. Larger flights of ducks were materializing out over the main lake. The flyout began.

The first bird of the morning was a pintail hen—not preferred. In this case, the light was still dim enough that I'd misjudged her for a drake. Only one per hunter was allowed in the Central Flyway. The pintail fell far enough out that I had to use the canoe for retrieval. With reps, the drill became more fluid, till it only took about five minutes from leaving to being back in the blind. Teal were on the move and flying by with regularity. I'd have been a fool not to take advantage of at least a couple. But the wife was expecting ducks to cook, so I needed to leave room for bigger ducks, too. I got a couple of teal in the bag and was able to retrieve them on foot.

A pair of pintails, hen and drake, flew practically in my face over the dekes. The drake was beautiful but now off-limits. As the morning pressed on, lots of teal passed by. I let them go. About ten o'clock or so, diver traffic was picking up. A flight of redheads came by out over the diver string from out of nowhere. They were out of range by the time I got my gun up, on the deck and moving fast. Not long after that a pair of canvasbacks came in, and I shot behind one. Heartbreak!

Bird traffic would pick up every fifteen minutes, it seemed. The problem with a lot of it was that it was almost all pintail! I'd never seen so many pintail in one place: huge flights of them. With my limit on pintail filled for the day, I was getting good at picking them out. Before packing up, I shot a young-of-the-year mallard drake and a Canada goose. What better note to end on? I could have hunted another two hours. With the last of the decoys loaded up, I paddled a course back to camp. Knowing I had one bird left in my limit, I kept the shotgun ready, just in case. Wouldn't you know it: I managed to sneak up on a lone wigeon drake and jump shoot him from the canoe within sight of camp!

Two hours later, the canoe was on the roof, trailer in tow, and I was headed south with ten days of duck-hunting memories in the bank. It had been everything I expected and so much more. The rhythm of the last ten days had been restorative. A hunt like this all comes down to timing. Throw it off

Canoes mean more access to ducks in Montana.

by any number of days, and all conditions could be off. Two weeks from that day, the first blizzard of late fall hit, with snow and subzero temperatures. All the water I hunted would be under ice and devoid of ducks. The coyote's howl would be lonely, the marsh frozen and silent. To witness such bounty and know it is all so fleeting, even though it is very much right there in front of you, is a reminder of the fragility and ever-changing nature of life. All good things come to an end.

REFERENCES

DeVoto, Bernard, ed. *The Journals of Lewis and Clark*. New York: Houghton-Mifflin, 1981.

Fifer, Barbara, and Joseph A. Mussulman. "George Drouillard: Hunter and Interpreter (1773–1810)." https://lewis-clark.org/members/george-drouillard.

Galloway, Colin G. "The Other Indians on the 1876 Campaign." In *Montana Legacy: Essays on History, People, and Place*, edited by Harry W. Fritz, Mary Murphy and Robert R. Swartout Jr., 27–41. Helena: Montana Historical Society Press, 2002.

Haines, Aubrey L., ed. *Osbourne Russell's Journal of a Trapper*. Lincoln: University of Nebraska Press, 1965.

Lane, Robert N. "The Remarkable Odyssey of Stream Access in Montana." *Public Land and Resources Law Review* 36, article 5 (July 2015): 71–171.

Montana State Legislature. *Montana Code Annotated 2023. Title 23, Chapter 2, Part 3, Recreational Use of Streams 23-2-302.* 2023.

Morgan, Dale A. *Jedediah Smith and the Opening of the West*. Lincoln: University of Nebraska Press, 1953,

Snow, John B. "The Godfather of Montana's Bighorn River." *Outdoor Life*. October 6, 2023.

Spritzer, Don. *Roadside History of Montana*. Missoula: Mountain Press Publishing, 1999.

U.S. Fish and Wildlife Service. "Red Rock Lakes." https://www.fws.gov.

Wemple, Matt. "Freezout Lake—A Habitat Gem: An Interview with Mark Schlepp." *Montana Sporting Journal*, 2013.

ABOUT THE AUTHOR

Matt Wemple is a lifelong avid outdoorsman and a published writer and photographer. Since 2005, his work has appeared in *Field & Stream*, *Sports Afield*, *Strung Sporting Journal*, *Bugle*, *Backcountry Journal*, *Fur-Fish-Game*, *Trapper & Predator Caller*, *Montana Sporting Journal*, *Traditional Bowhunter* and *Mule Deer Foundation Magazine*. Matt writes monthly for the *Lewis and Clark Journal* based in Three Forks, Montana. In addition to *Montana Duck Hunting Tales*, he has authored three books: *The Duck Camp*, *To Hunt Ducks* and *Headwaters Country: Everyday Life in Southwest Montana*. Professionally, Matt has spent his entire adult life in the military and law enforcement. He works full time as a Montana game warden and serves in the Montana National Guard. See more of his work at mattwempleoutdoors.com.

Layout blinds are essential for Montana's shortgrass prairie.